in the mind of the writer

nancy dean

Hunter College

canfield press   san francisco
a department of harper & row, publishers, inc.
new york   evanston   london

to
ella lang dean
among the finest and gentlest of teachers

Book Design by Deborah Bragman

In the Mind of the Writer

Copyright © 1973 by Nancy Dean

For information address Harper & Row, Publishers, Inc.
10 East 53rd Street, New York, N.Y. 10022

International Standard Book Number: 0-06-382553-8
Library of Congress Catalog Card Number: 72-9382
    73 74 75 10 9 8 7 6 5 4 3 2 1

contents

preface

Why should anyone bother to write? Cassette recorders are now in widespread use to transcribe records, lectures, interviews, and a variety of sounds. You can send a tape instead of a letter to a parent, or talk to a tape instead of a friend. Why struggle with grammar and the search for the right word when it is so much easier to relax and speak what comes into your mind?

In a certain sense the tape recorder is, despite its technological magic, more primitive than writing. It offers us only what the cave man heard when men spoke—the human voice with grunt one preceding mumble fifteen by a few seconds. But the reader of a written speech can review all parts of a passage still in time, but almost all at once. He can see quickly that idea *A* does not lead on to idea *B,* that the conclusion is incomplete, and that idea *D* was not explained.

How many times have you been impressed with a persuasive speaker who seemed sincere, looked honest, spoke directly and, you thought, clearly? When that handsome and persuasive speaker sat down, have you ever wondered what his basic ideas were? If his individual points were clear, have you ever wondered what the connection between them was? Often the hypnotic speaker wins us for all the wrong reasons—because he is vigorous, direct, convinced—not because his ideas are good; and when he stops talking, the ideas have drifted off through the open window. Were they logical? Would they have withstood shrewd questions? The quick-minded listener may have some sinister suspicions, but the speaker himself may be the last one to know the weakness of his logic.

You may feel that it is easier to talk than to write, but if you think about it for a moment, you will realize that you mean it is easier to talk vaguely and get away with it than it is to write illogically and escape observation. But self-observation is what matters. If you can see your own slips from logic and good sense more clearly in a written passage than in an oral one, writing is more useful for your self-knowledge than the tape recorder is.

Writing is, in fact, one of the swiftest means to know yourself. For the student, that is its greatest justification. Because writing feels more unnatural than speaking, though both are learned behaviors, the writer pauses, searches for the word to express his meaning. If he is honest, the struggle is hard, because as he gropes for the right word he discovers what he does not mean. As he selects the precise word, he discovers his own meaning. It is not that he knows what he wishes to say but can't say it. Rather, he learns what he thinks as he chooses his words.

Any sort of writing with the exception of laundry lists, grocery lists, and "things to be done" offers challenging possibilities to say accurately what you mean. Fifteen minutes of writing at night in a journal can provide regular practice in introspection that is even better than talking to a friend. In writing to yourself, because you know the event you describe, you are challenged to complete honesty, hence accuracy of expression. In this way, writing can be a mirror of the self, which can provide insight without the flattery or distortion that the kind judgments or misjudgments of friends provide.

The best reason to write, then, is to know your own thought and to understand yourself. The effort to say what you mean clarifies your meaning to yourself. This small book is to aid the writer's personal search on the assumption that some of the very best teaching is self-teaching and that if a person studies his own writing and thinking he can become his own best critic.

The book has been written in the form of a dialogue. The questions asked are, in most part, those that have been asked by students of their teachers for many years. The answers are as direct and honest as I could make them, but they express a personal view of writing: that it is best when it is clear, simple, precise, and that it is worth doing mainly because it forces us to know ourselves better and so pushes us to understand others better.

My own thanks are due to many fine teachers of writing who have influenced, surely, thousands of students: Anne Walker and Elizabeth C. Sanderson, J. Max Patrick, I. A. Richards, and Helen D. Lockwood.

Acknowledgments, no matter how grateful, can never be accurate and complete, because all living words, read or heard, begin to grow within one's own thinking; I wish, however, to acknowledge the influence of books, colleagues, friends, and perhaps most of all, my own students, whose challenging vitality has enriched my own experience more than they know. This book is written for their use. I want to thank particularly these students who contributed their own writing and their suggestions to this book: Karen Abbott, Mary Bunyea, Sue Chin, Pedro Cortes, Carl Harris, Mary McCarthy, Brian McCormack, Joann Olbrich, Barbara Otremba, Janice White. Finally, I owe thanks to Jenelle Wood for her careful typing and to Myrna Harrison whose reading and shrewd suggestions improved the book's structure.

New York City
September 1972   NANCY DEAN

the language of the paper

the case
for a
paper language

Should I Write as I Speak?

Some people say so. They say that writing should be natural, should flow easily, should seem unstrained or even casual. That loose expression ''write as you speak'' asserts an ideal standard, that writing should appear simple and plain like the language of speech. One writer who writes in a beautifully plain, uncluttered style that seems utterly natural told me that he had worked on his small book for two years and that he had written each page thirty times.

What seems natural, simple, and clear is achieved with great effort. The doctrine of natural writing does not withstand scrutiny. First, it is not natural to write, or to read either. Writing is a product

3

of civilization, and prose, more than poetry, is produced only in a long-settled civilization. Second, what seems natural in reading and writing is a product of custom. If everyone said "gobbledy" before every sentence for long enough, it would be accepted, and in a generation or so, children would be reprimanded for refusing to say their gobbledies properly.

The spoken language provides only a general pattern for the written language; if it were followed literally, there would be at least four different written languages. The language spoken with close friends would be recorded in written words as monosyllabic, comfortable grunts of agreement or displeasure: "Um . . . yeah . . . wha?" and so forth. Hemingway's clipped dialogue of his best days records an ideal conversation, not the realistic speech so often praised. An actual record of close friends conversing would include miles of half-formulated, badly articulated thoughts, but friends understand one another. They read each other's minds, and a good part of the pleasure of friendships is in the chance to relax, knowing one will be understood without the endless effort to express meaning precisely.

For acquaintances there is the slangy shorthand of "beautiful" and "like wow," or whatever the present common coin may be. Like the formal "How are you today?" these phrases merely admit that friendship is assumed. They are not to be answered or understood literally. If people wrote as they spoke in this language of comfortable acquaintanceship, the language would be too vague and half-formulated to express ideas adequately. The language would wave an arm in the direction of some general idea down the block, but it could not put its hand on an idea and offer it to a reader.

The language spoken to those who are in authority—bosses, teachers, deans—will not work either. It is too restricted, too evasive. It refuses to communicate anything intimate or profound. The language spoken to parents is too babyish, usually too lacking in idea-content. Like the Turkish students who can express themselves beautifully at levels of high abstraction in English but not in Turkish—because they have studied philosophy, political science, and English in English, but not in their parent language—people of all ages rarely can speak with parents at their present level of intellectual growth. Having spoken for years at home about behavior, permissions, events, gossip, it is difficult to begin speaking with parents about ideas and problems.

4

In fact, if we wrote as we speak, we would not have the vocabulary or the complexity of sentence structure to permit the expression of difficult ideas or their relationships. As a person's reading vocabulary develops far beyond the vocabulary he uses in casual conversations, so his understanding of the complexities of sentence and paragraph structure usually outstrips the language he speaks. The old languages spoken to friends, family and so-called superiors become inadequate. The student begins to crave a more precise self-expression than most casual speech can achieve. He needs to create a new language that permits a more complete expression of ideas for his school and college writing, yet if he were to speak the new language now, his friends would think he was showing off. Often the development of his articulateness begins to be inhibited by his friends' opinions. This dilemma can be evaded neatly by writing, and the new language, fashioned for school and college writing, may become the regular language spoken in adulthood. Most people, however, maintain quite a disparity between the language they speak (to friends, acquaintances), the language they read (newspapers, magazines, biographies, detective stories, novels, histories), and the language they write (bills, memos, reports, letters). Homogeneity of language would be tedious and ineffective; this diversity of spoken and written languages permits a range of communication.

What Should This New Paper Language Be Like?

It should be more objective, more correct, and more articulate than the English that most people speak. Subjectivity, incorrectness, and inarticulateness, however, are evils only because they obscure the author's meaning; they are not in themselves evil, and they can even be effective conversation. As there is no one perfect way to organize a paper, there is no one perfect paper language. There is, however, one goal any writer can steer by: clarity of communication. The best language is the most effective one. The elegant speech appropriate to the university forum should be put aside in speaking to children. But in the writing done in schools and colleges, the subject, primarily—not the audience—determines the need for a new language. The subject requires the language to be more objective, more articulate, and more correct. The loose, private, casual language will not permit the writer to come through loud and clear. Like a bad telephone line with static and blank-outs, lost syllables and faraway voices, the inadequate language prevents the author's thoughts from reaching the mind of the reader.

It is true also that the author's thoughts may not be clearly formulated until he tries to express them; he then realizes their formlessness and begins to strain to determine what he means. When students say, "I know what I want to say, but I just can't say it," they are probably grappling with a half-formed thought. They may need time to work out what they mean, because even confusion can be clearly expressed. Language can point to a problem, define it, cite its sources of difficulty, and say, "Here is a mystery, and here is a confusion." The process of defining one's own thoughts —attempting to express the thought with more objectivity, more correctness, more articulateness—leads to increased clarity of thought as well as to increased clarity of expression, thus clearing up that telephone line to the reader.

Why Be More Objective? What Is Wrong with Being Personal?

There is nothing wrong with written expression that is personal and highly subjective. In the autobiography, that genre of writing based on self-revelation, subjectivity is often useful. In that genre, a work sometimes increases in value if the audience believes the writer "reveals all." In a short story, an event may be seen through the eyes of one character and told by him. That use of "point of view" requires sharp subjectivity, the personal revelation of what that character might feel or think during the event described. In contemporary journalism writers frequently present themselves as witnesses. Their work gains impact because they assert what they have seen, experienced, reacted to, or cared about. Their person-alities as observers of life add immediacy and vividness, as well as their personal perspectives, to the piece. Although this I-was-there manner is not always appropriate for the subjects of research papers, there are a few writers who can give a detective-story zip to their retelling of research—people like Alvin Toffler, Isaac Asimov, Leonard Cottrell, Leslie Hotson, and Richard Altick. These writers in social and natural science, archeology, and English literary history are, in a certain sense, gifted storytellers.

On the other hand, in writing for classes in school or college, the student should not presume that his teacher is someone who will enjoy hearing about everything but the subject of the paper. Many students assume that their material is dull and that they should liven it up with contemporary references to riots, bikinis, TV, or dope addiction. They presume that their own paper is some bad-tasting medicine that should be sweetened with something, anything but their own ideas, which they presume are not worth hearing. The assumption here is wrong on both counts: there is no bad-tasting medicine, and the most interesting thing about the paper, its focus or purpose, is presentation of ideas, not of way-out comparisons. In fact, the rapid, clear presentation of ideas is any paper's best sweetening.

The student's job is to have ideas about the material and then to present them rapidly, dropping out fillers and padders, so that the paper will seem to move quickly from idea to idea. The paper on Huckleberry Finn might say by implication, "Huck gradually developed toward maturity through the novel. These events, illustrations, critical evaluations support that statement." The research paper on ecology might assert indirectly, "Recycling or constructive use of waste materials is vital. Here are some examples of what the Japanese and the Scandinavians are doing to solve the problem." The thesis then will be shown to be valid, not because the writer feels it to be so or wishes it were valid, but because his evidence argues persuasively that it is so. In that sense, the writer's feelings may inspire and motivate the paper and its views, but direct expression of those feelings does not always strengthen the paper.

If I Feel It, Why Can't I Say So?

Since everything stated in a paper that is not enclosed in quotation marks is presumed to be the author's opinion and his language, there is no need to say "I feel" or "I think" unless special emphasis is desired. Most papers, in fact, should be directed toward presenting the author's thoughts and ideas, buttressed by illustrations, evidence, quotations, facts, critical opinions—whatever pieces of putty, mortar, plastic, steel, and string he can find. At times, you may find yourself in a corner, having, for example, presented at length the ideas of someone whose views you do not share. How do you make it clear that you, as author, disagree? There are polite ways to convey disagreement. You can say, "On the other hand," and proceed with your rebuttal. You do not have to say, "However, I think," or, "This author is a ninny as any intelligent person can see."

If the Author Can't Say "I," Where Is He?

Does the author become invisible or turn into some kind of committee standing behind the typewriter saying, "It is thought:" (By whom? All of us here in committee? We, the editor of this important journal? We, the Duke of Normandy?) The author can say "I" if he thinks it adds a significant emphasis, but a belief that there is no other way to state his conviction is no reason to say "I." There is always another way, and without using the passive construction. In looking for that other way to assert what he sees, the writer will become a better observer, not to mention a better writer. The writer is, in fact, omnipresent, hovering over his material, arranging its order to be more persuasive, introducing his quotations so that his reader will understand their pertinence, preparing his reader to be convinced by the time he reaches the final, clinching arguments. The logical line of the arguments and the selection of material are his. In fact, as selector, commentator, arranger, he dominates his paper. The problem is to let the material appear to persuade without that egomaniacal "I" talking all the time.

When the "I" is taken away, writers often slip into the passive form. Having spoken with "I" all their lives, naturally they feel without a handrail in a rocking boat. Or taking fright, they hide behind the pompous language that they think must be right. The properly self-respecting freshman will say directly:

> I really think that Hamlet doesn't put off taking action. When I think of every event he was supposed to act in and didn't, I can think of a good reason for his not acting. For instance, when he could have killed the king while Claudius was praying, he didn't kill him because he thought if he did the king's spirit would go straight to heaven. As he says, "Why, this is hire and salary not revenge."

The junior who has been told not to use I, not to use contractions in formal writing, not to end with prepositions, not to develop ideas too fast in paragraphs might understandably feel afraid to say much at all and might end by saying something like this:

> It is rather universally thought that Hamlet delays revenging his father's "unnatural murder" because he is enveloped in self-delusion or is an inveterate procrastinator. However, it will be seen that in those events in which action might have been possible there are mitigating factors to be found for Hamlet's not acting when it is thought by many that he should have acted.

A simple style between those two extremes needs to be used. That "committee" in the junior's paragraph—the "it" doing all the thinking and finding—is as exhausting as most committees are. Use the active voice and the direct declarative statement in the third person.

> Although many critics insist that Hamlet "is a man who could not make up his mind," one who delays facing an issue, Hamlet does not procrastinate. In fact, for every moment that critics say he "should" have acted, there are excellent reasons for his inactivity.

Many students feel that a paragraph of this sort is arrogant. It asserts as fact what is interpretation. That is true. Still, if the writer recognizes his obligation to support every assertion or generalization, there is no arrogance in making a statement he will sustain with evidence. Students should not consider it arrogant to state what they see. As you stand by the window observing the rain falling, it is not arrogant to state, "It is raining."

Naturally, many students feel that if they make a flat assertion using a firm declarative sentence and they turn out to be wrong they will be embarrassed. If the evidence supporting a generalization is not adequate, is misdirected or illogical, these are other problems. If the text has been misinterpreted, that is still another problem. But none of these is helped or corrected by language like the junior's with his committee of "it" and his passive voice. His language can make the whole passage obscure and will not help him work out the textual problems. The clear, declarative statement using the third person ("he," "she," "it," "Hamlet"), the active voice ("he sees," not "it is seen" or "it is thought") can, in its objective form, still state the writer's subjective views.

9

Does Objective Mean Pompous?

Most students would respond promptly that objectivity does not mean pomposity, yet in aiming for the objective style, the young writer often overreaches and finds himself giving this kind of an account of Mary:

> It has been reported that a young female individual going by the appellation Mary was recently viewed to have been accompanied or perhaps pursued to her local institution of lower education by an infantile member of that wide variety of cud-chewing mammals termed sheep. Its actions on that occasion were in violation of the local ordinances regarding presences of domesticated creatures within the classroom structure. Further, the local regulations against such activities were amply vindicated by the excessive levity demonstrated by the kindergarten children.

Students are less likely to be guilty of presenting such a demented account of Mary than their teachers are, and there are many reasons for this, most of which come down to self-protection. Not wishing to appear foolish, naïve, or simple, the writer reaches for impressive language to protect himself. No one will call him stupid or uneducated (although he may be called a bore). Readers who admit to finding stilted language tedious may be admitting that they do not understand the writer's ideas; criticism, therefore, is rarely voiced. Few writers for professional journals try seriously to avoid jargon, fearing that they might be called naïve or unprofessional. This is just one example of the timidity that makes a hardworking professional person write the language he would hate to read. With teachers so bullied by their peers, it is hardly surprising that their students tend, as they travel through school, to become writers of jargon also. But jargon is not objectivity.

The student who wishes to avoid the subjectivity of saying "I think Huck Finn is" will often swerve to the jargon of "It is thought that Huckleberry Finn is," when all he needs is the declarative third person, "Huck Finn is." Simple third-person assertions place emphasis where it should be—on the material out there, what it is, what it looks like, what it does, how it is put together.

That the master of the heroic couplet, Alexander Pope, aspired to correctness surprises no one. Correctness seems an acceptable goal for an eighteenth-century writer, but how can anyone offer it as a goal for a twentieth-century writer in a decade that questions all customs and values?

What Kind of Correctness Makes Any Sense in Writing?

The writer needs to be correct, not to be well-behaved or proper, but to be understood. Confusions of communication are based, usually, on the writer's incorrect grammar or incorrect punctuation, or on the reader's inability or unwillingness to read carefully. Before the terms "lady" and "gentleman" passed into disrepute, variations on this sentence appeared: "A lady never insults anyone unintentionally." The point of the saying was that a lady's manners were so good that she would never, by unconscious lapse, insult anyone. If one were insulted by a lady, then, one could be sure that the slight was intended. Writing requires this same total consciousness in order to avoid the unintended obscurity or ambiguity. Good reading, too, requires this alertness to punctuation, connotation, and denotation. Many students repeat ideas as though they did not expect to be listened to the first or the second time. Common observation suggests that most people do not expect to be listened to attentively, and we all tend to repeat until the other person comments, nods, or indicates that he has, in fact, absorbed what we thought escaped him. Writers cannot waste time in repetitions such as, "She didn't understand, like she didn't get it," in which the clause following the ungrammatical "like" merely repeats "understand."

Grammatical correctness is vital, not just because status is involved and an intelligent person may be underestimated if his grammar is bad, but for a more important reason: because incorrect grammar communicates ideas less effectively than correct grammar does. Sometimes the confusions are like static and merely annoy the careful reader by deflecting his attention from the writer's ideas.

"While walking down the street, the house was robbed." The confusion here is amusing. The reader wonders how fast the house was walking. But in that momentary deflecting of interest, the excitement that the writer may have been working to create has been dissipated.

"In considering the Holy Sonnets John Donne also wrote sermons, satires, and love poems." While he was considering the Holy

Sonnets? Pretty busy man, the reader thinks. This sentence was meant as a transition, permitting the author to shift from subject *A* (Holy Sonnets) to subject *B* (sermons, satires, and love poems). Which are the subjects? Who does the author mean is doing the considering?

"In the throes of gardening the bird flew by." Who or what is said to be gardening? Because no one would be likely to consider the bird busily raking leaves, there is no confusion here. The ridiculousness of what is stated is obvious; the writer must have meant something other than he said. Suppose the subject were less clear and more important to national affairs: "In the act of spying the Russian missionary walked out of the room." If the writer did not mean to say that the Russian missionary was spying, he has still precipitated an international crisis. The obvious noun modified by "in the act of spying" is the missionary. The writer may have meant, "While I was in the act of spying the Russian missionary walked out of the room." Too bad. What his words said has made one Russian furious.

The sentence about the bird and the one about the Russian missionary have precisely the same structure and defect: prepositional phrase modifying the wrong noun. The defect of the first sentence was obvious because of its silly content, but that of the second could not be readjusted by the reader through thinking, as he did about the bird (a bird can't garden), "A Russian missionary couldn't spy!"

Similarly, the error of an ambiguous reference can be important—quite upsetting if the reader wants to understand the news: "President Nixon said to his first in command that he had violated the Bill of Rights." Who is said to have violated the Bill of Rights, the president or his first in command? How might the sentence be corrected?

"He really loved school and didn't miss a day for thirteen years which made his sister jealous." That particular use of "which" would be of interest to the sister. Is she jealous because he loved school and she did not, or because he had not missed a day for thirteen years and she had? If the writer insists that each of his nouns and noun substitutes ("he," "she," "it," "who," "which," "what," "this," "that," "the same," "each") refers to a specific noun or pronoun he will not commit this error in any of its forms. Attention to these reference words will help your understanding of all kinds of reading.

"The dancer made some beautiful leaps despite the pain in her foot which moved the audience to ecstatic applause." Did the audience enjoy the pain in her foot? The "which" is too far from the noun to which it presumably refers.

"Everyone, to express their concern, wrote angry letters to his congressman." Words such as "everyone," "each," "every," "none," "either," "neither" usually take a singular verb. The writer of that sentence has said that everyone wrote his congressman expressing the concern of some other people. Did he mean to say that, or did he mean that everyone expressed his own concern by writing letters to his own congressman? If he meant the second, "their" of "their concern" should be changed to "his." In context the sentence might have been clearer. The writer might have meant that some Alaskan citizens were speaking up for the Eskimos who were not at the moment writing their congressman. Although the context (those sentences surrounding a sentence) can clear up confusions, a writer would be embarrassed to learn that his readers had to extract his meaning from context because his word choice was so inexact.

Is Grammatical Correctness the Only Kind I Should Worry About?

Punctuation, which, like grammar, is so often considered by students to be fussy, trivial, and unimportant, can be as significant as word choice. Of course, a line of commas and semicolons without words would not communicate much. No one would say that these slight touches of ink above and below the line of words mean more than words, but they do affect the meanings of words significantly. The apostrophe for possession, for example, begins to leave the classroom because it is said, by nameless villains, to be trivial.

> My mothers hats are all flowery. (Makes no sense. Why?)
> My mothers' hats are all ugly. (Says something about father. What?)
> My mother's hats are splendid. (Even if the sentence is untrue, its punctuation is correct. Why?)

Some would say that since one person is speaking and each person has only one mother no apostrophe of possession is needed at all in those sentences. At present the apostrophe alters the meaning of the word it accompanies; "mother's hat" ('s) means the hat worn by one mother, but "mothers' hat" (s') means the one hat worn or owned by more than one mother, an unlikely situation. Consider the implications of this passage: "The General Assembly was quiet. All heads turned. The ambassador ('s, s' ?) portfolios were empty." Granting that every ambassador has more than one portfolio, this serious situation concerns one ambassador or many—depending on the position of the apostrophe.

"He reported to the police that his girls rings and necklaces were taken." How would you punctuate that sentence to mean that he had one girl? How would you punctuate it to say that he had several?

The rule of the apostrophe of possession is essentially that the writer leaves the word as it is in his context, singular or plural. To the singular he adds 's; to the plural he adds '. "The house's new coat of paint" is singular. "Their houses' new coats of paint" is plural. But there are plurals formed with *n* that take 's, like men's ties, women's dresses, children's jungle gyms.

How Else Can Punctuation Be Important?

The comma that indicates the <u>nonrestrictive clause</u> is another example of significant punctuation. One sentence may be punctuated with or without that comma and have two quite different meanings, for example:

- Young teachers who remember vividly the painful moments of their own school days are likely to be effective in communicating with their students. (No comma before "who" and after "days".)
- Young teachers, who remember vividly the painful moments of their own school days, are likely to be effective in communicating with their students. (With comma before "who" and after "days".)

The first sentence says that the young teachers who remember are likely to be effective. It recognizes that not all young teachers do recall their youthful miseries. The second sentence says that young teachers as a group are likely to be effective. It presumes that the memories of all young teachers remain vivid.

The additional clause, the one that adds nonessential material to the sentence, is called "nonrestrictive" and is separated by commas as if it were parenthetical. The comma is not used for the vital, identifying (restrictive) clause.

"Her father, who works at a bank, hates his job." Since she has only one father, he is identified sufficiently by "her father." In relation to the identification of the subject, the working at the bank is additional and unnecessary. Of course, the information is of interest in that it may explain his hatred of the job, but, grammatically speaking, the information is irrelevant to the use of the comma for the nonrestrictive clause. Another example:

- He rushed onto the field to help the players who had been knocked down by the goal posts.
- He rushed onto the field to help the players, who had been knocked down by the goal posts.

Did he help only those few players who had been knocked down, or did he help all the players (all having been knocked down by the goal posts)?

In the first sentence, the clause "who . . . posts" identifies those particular players whom he helped and indicates that other players were present but were not felled by the goal posts. The clause is necessary to the identification of the ones he helped. The comma is therefore omitted. The second sentence says that he helped the players, all of them. The "who . . . post" clause is additional, not necessary to identify further the people whom he helped. They have been identified by the word *players*. More examples of the comma that signals the nonrestrictive clause:

- Alex Howard, who wrote that marvelous description about living under the sea, is at work on a novel now. (Commas are needed because the subject is identified by his name, and the *who* clause, although welcome information perhaps, is not needed to identify Alex Howard.)
- I know two Alex Howards. The Alex Howard who wrote that marvelous description about living under the sea is at work on a novel now. (This time, more than the name was needed to identify the Alex Howard meant.)
- The dog that I had seen earlier gasping by the roadside trotted

toward me, head up and tail wagging. (The clause "that I had seen earlier" is necessary to the identification, so it is not enclosed in commas.)

- Harry's dog, which I had seen earlier gasping by the roadside, trotted . . . wagging. ("Harry's dog" identifies the dog. What if Harry had seven dogs? How should the sentence be written using a restrictive clause?)

Decide about the punctuation of each of these:

- The contract that I mentioned was carelessly written.
- The contract which was carelessly written left the movie star penniless.
- The new car which is parked outside is a gift to him from the village.
- The car that is parked outside has traveled 100,000 miles and looks it.
- Alice quietly answered the woman who was sputtering obscenities and then gestured to the intern.
- The intern who was new to the ward came forward promptly.

Think of nonrestrictive clauses as nonnecessary to the identification of the noun modified and restrictive clauses as necessary for the identification of the noun, requiring free connection with the noun without the obstruction of commas. If "that" is reserved for restrictive clauses and "which" for nonrestrictive clauses, written work can be kept trimmer; which's seem to add bulk.

Restrictive and nonrestrictive phrases operate by the same rule for punctuation that clauses do. Punctuate these:

- A car without a tire won't help us now.
- Our car without a tire since the accident can't help us now.
- All his shoes with good heels and soles or not were thrown out.
- "But I liked them," he wailed. "Shoes with good soles shouldn't be tossed out."
- The girl looking through the binoculars gave a shout to her friends.
- Mary Ann watching the planet through the telescope kept thinking about space travel.

What Do You Mean, "Be More Articulate" on Paper?

Most people communicate well with their friends and family. They may not agree with one another, but they know each other's meaning. Custom, gestures, facial expressions, vocal intonations are all there to help us understand an old friend or a family member. Frequently, on meeting a new friend, we make the same mistakes in evaluating him or her that we can make in reading an essay written by a stranger. We listen to what the new friend says, but lacking familiarity with his ways, we misinterpret a joke for a serious statement or sarcasm for criticism. His words alone did not communicate.

The language of the essay cannot rest on familiarity; it is written for one or more strangers. It must say what it means and cannot depend on casual, undefined references. It cannot assume that the reader shares the writer's attitudes toward anything, from ball teams to capitalism. It would not have the vocabulary to discourse about the subjects of many essays if it were, literally, the language that most people speak. But most important, it would be too imprecise because it would be loaded with clichés and vague phrases.

What Is a Cliché?

Although the *Oxford English Dictionary* says a cliché is "a metal stereotype of a wood engraving used to print from," the term "cliché" usually is applied metaphorically to speech and writing, to those phrases that have been repeated so often that they may as well be printed all together in a block, like "dryasdust," "thisdayandage," or "youneverknow" and "timewilltell." Ideas as well as phrases can become stereotyped. They are like inseparable clusters formed on a subject. There, they congeal, and it takes years of education and introspection to dissolve them. "All boys love football." "Germans are very mechanical." "Girls can't do math." Clichés of thought are often expressed in clichés of speech. Hundreds of commencement speeches turn on "the threshold of the new day" theme. "Young people are the hope of the world stepping out on the long journey of life." Granted that graduation does mark the beginning of new experiences; that young people are educable and do offer more hope for constructive changes, usually, but not always, than their parents do; that platitudes often have a basic truth—still, the trite language permits little new thinking and tends to prevent it.

Language is diminished by any phrase that expects or encourages indifference. Phrases like "at long last," "last but not least," "first, last, and always," "day and age," "here and there," "far and near," and "hither and yon" are dull because they are so predictable. Say "hither," nudge a friend, and he will say "yon." The predictableness of the phrase loses the reader's attention. If the reader drifts off often enough, "the game is lost," and you can never persuade him of anything; his mind is not with you.

> **At long last the sun rose; a new day broke over Tonowanda. Not that Jean had much hope that any light would be shed on her troubles, but she did feel better.**

"A new day broke" is one of the dullest ways to describe—what? That is the trouble. The writer was not interested in describing the day. The phrase was used merely to indicate that time had passed or to say "the next day." The rising of morning light needs to be described fully and well, or it should not be mentioned. In the example, it is a kind of code for "and then" or "next day." The "shedding of light on" anything is pure cliché. Clichés in light imagery abound. But the poets can bring off a light image freshly: Milton's blind Samson, captive and in fetters, "Dark, dark, dark, amid the blaze of noon"; or Dylan Thomas' powerful "Do not go gentle into that good night/ Rage, rage against the dying of the light." But in these illustrations the light/dark imagery is tightly bound to the meaning of the work. It is not merely ornament. Whenever you feel like saying "shed light on," substitute a direct phrase or sentence. Describe the troubles that need resolving: "She did not expect to find her lost engagement ring or keep the loss from Joel, who was coming to visit, but at least her fever had passed." This reworking of the "at long last" sentence in the example may not be great prose, but it is, at least, specific.

The great poets, the Bible, popular songs, advertising commercials—the sources of clichés are . . . (fill in "legion" or "too numerous to mention"). Poor *Hamlet* has been praised more for its quotations, perhaps, than for its structure: "brevity is the soul of wit"; "to thine own self be true," taken from that old hypocrite Polonius; "how noble a work is man"; "more than kin and less than kind"; "more matter and less art"; "something rotten in the State of Denmark." How many children have been patronized or told to be quiet, with Pope's fine phrase, "A little learning is a dangerous thing?" But Pope's finish urges respect for learning.

Drink deep, or taste not the Pierian spring:
There shallow draughts intoxicate the brain,
And drinking largely sobers us again.[1]

Without discrimination, taste, or respect for the meaning of the original, effective phrases are drawn from literature into our current language and used without comprehension until they become invisible. This repetition of phrases and lifting great sayings out of context has been going on, presumably, since men first lived together long enough to listen to one another. Not that one should approve a practice because it is incorrigible, but it is consoling to realize that our own period is not remarkably undiscriminating. A bold baron of the medieval period is said to have urged his men on in battle, saying something like, "Onward men. It is well known to be harder to keep what one has gained than to win. But keep we must," etc. He seems to have thought that he cited scripture, but he was quoting Ovid's lore about winning and keeping a sweetheart. Our misuse can hardly be worse than that.

Are All Clichés Taken from Formal Sources, like Literature and the Bible?

Some clichés are metaphors that have died from exhaustion but must have seemed imaginative once. "His telegram was a bolt from the blue." "His telegram was a surprise" would be more stirring than that limp lightning bolt. "Fresh as paint, as usual, she answered back." "The easterner, green as grass, climbed into the saddle." "The turtle was dead as a doornail." It would be worth research to know why doornails are so often cited as dead. Alliteration, that repetition of the initial consonant, may be the only reason for "dead as a doornail," unless there is humor intended in the notion that doornails never lived. What, then, could be deader than a dead doornail? The point here is that listeners no longer hear or think about the exhausted metaphor or simile. Avoid the problem by substituting newer comparisons or use simple statements.

But What's Wrong with Clichés? I Ignore Them; They Don't Hurt Anyone.

Most discussions of clichés seem to imply that triteness or predictability is the central reason that clichés should be avoided. Clichés are dangerous because they keep writers and readers from thinking beyond them, because they half conceal thought while seeming to express it.

"But, you see, this sort of visitor will disturb our way of life," he said soberly, and all the elders nodded.

What does the speaker mean by "way of life"? An elder should ask. What is the speaker's way of life: smuggling? white slave trade? quiet dope addiction? One should know the referent before agreeing about ways of life. "What do you mean by 'our way of life'?" might seem a silly question, but the vagueness of the cliché permits any possibility. Unfortunately few people insist on definitions of this kind of cliché.

"Surely, if we all live it, no one here needs to have our way of life explained. Or can it be that you do not share our way of life?"

One could be in trouble with the neighbors very quickly.

The undefined phrase is dangerous; habits of thought encouraged by frequent uses of clichés hinder mental development. To think of "turning a new page" or "a new leaf" in your life's story is an unconstructive habit of mind because your life is not a romance, to be told by a cozy fireside.

Proverbial wisdom also becomes cliché and prevents independent thinking. "Opportunity only knocks once" is an untruth. In fact, opportunity is only in attitude. It may be said to be knocking every instant, but let an OPPORTUNITY—a new job, a new invitation—be offered, and countless friends will be on the telephone saying that "Opportunity only knocks once." They may even say, "there is a tide in the affairs of men which, taken at the flood leads on to fortune. . . ," etc., not knowing that Brutus was soundly defeated in the battle of Philippi after his great speech.

Clichés come in different packages: trite phrases, proverbs, tired similes and metaphors, alliterative phrases. If you care about your own growth, they are to be avoided (fill in "like the plague") not just because they are dull and the reader stops listening, or because they diminish the language by encouraging indifference to it, although those reasons are strong ones. Clichés hinder the development of the writer's own thinking, if he accepts them and uses them. If he writes about the "threshold of life" and "a fine representative of our way of life," he is leaving his own ideas unexamined. The cliché permits, even encourages, indifference to both language and under-standing because it is so easy to reach for that trusted (fill in "tried and true") phrase. When we choose the ready-made phrase, we are dozing over life and experience. Use of the cliché is a genuine evil because it influences the writer's and the reader's habits of thought, and through this influence actually nurtures insensitivity to living.

style

Up to this time, the discussion of language has turned upon the author's attempt to say what he means, but to persuade others to agree requires other skills. The author must consider his own relation to the audience and to his material, thoughtfully. His expression of that relation will be in the words he selects, his chosen style, for that particular work. The style he chooses will affect his audience's response to the work. It may lead the audience toward acceptance or rejection of what he says.

What Is Style?

Before considering style in writing, consider it in dress. The young woman who chooses jeans and a simple shirt to wear to school is announcing that she wishes to be casual. If jeans are the accepted dress at her school, she is announcing that she is not competing to look the smartest or sleekest. She may be expressing, as well, her wish to dress like others, to be accepted by them, or her wish to be discreet, unobserved, even ignored. One cannot be dogmatic about what dress reveals about personality, but it is rarely insignificant, and it can be telling. As the black leather jacket, motorcycle boots, and military bearing announce, "I am tough," so the loose, long hair and the poverty-stricken look associated with hippies announce, "Materialistic values disgust me."

Although some people hold to one style of dress, many cultivate a variety of styles. The proper-looking lawyer who dresses impeccably to go to work in a well-pressed dark gray suit, a navy tie, and polished black shoes may collapse into gorgeously messy shirts and dungarees for weekends. He needs the contrast, for one thing. The shirts and dungarees are appropriate to his weekend chaos and the electric guitar twanging from his apartment, for another.

Style is with us everywhere, announcing its intentions in dress, speech, music. Almost everyone uses or responds to styles, whether or not he is conscious of doing so. Listen to the background music in television commercials to hear a stylistic commentary on the commercial messages. The lyric purity of the music in the background of the cigarette commercial is meant to convince the gullible that the cigarette is as pure and fresh as a summer day in spring. Flute music and twittering birds are used as background for commercials for burial plots and funeral services. The musical commentary is meant by its style to convince the listener of the delicacy and understanding with which his grief will be treated, presumably. The impassioned swelling of Rachmaninoff during the soap commercial as the simple druggist and the middle-aged spinster discover their passion in lather is meant to contrast amusingly the grandiose romantic music and the mundane romance. Music itself can have stylistic variations. For example, popular songs and some operas contain folk music themes, and there is a martial style in some Christian hymns, like "Onward Christian Soldiers," and in some symphonic music.

In speech, style is more difficult to understand because most people think they just "talk"; they are not aware that all speech is in some style. Observe your own speech. Boys may hear themselves talking slangier and tougher in the gym than they do, for example, in the classroom. To them, the less articulate language, which sounds to an outsider like a great blur of lingo and clichés, may seem freer and more individualistic than the more formal language approved by adults. The point is that the variety indicates use, however unconscious, of style in speech.

What Is Style in Speech, Exactly?

Style is the words actually chosen, like the items of clothing, which all together convey an impression or, as the phrase goes, "present an image." Style is almost as visible in language as it is in dress or painting or music. Where milk is delivered to houses, often a note must be left for the milkman. As the lawyer's correct legal plumage would be foolish for the way he spends his weekends, a formal style of writing would be pretty silly for the note to the milkman:

> Dear Mr. Milkman:
> It is of the utmost necessity that this house request of you an additional pint of cream upon your next delivery. Unfortunately, it was not possible for your last delivery to be accepted and paid for owing to the sudden absence of my husband whose plane was hijacked to Cuba. He will endeavor to fulfill our monetary obligations promptly.
> Thank you for your indulgence,
> Mrs. Mary Formal

The milkman would have to appear in a tuxedo to deliver milk to that house. The style of most notes to milkmen is brief bulletin or telegram style.

> 1 more pt. milk, please. Will pay next week.

The style of the letter home is similar to postcard style, like this:

> Had a real good time at Ralph's but had to leave early. Test tomorrow. It would be great if Teddy could send his old track shoes to me. Well, it's late now.
> Love to all,
> Tom

Journalists sometimes deliberately adopt an informal, casual style. Consider this paragraph, taken from the latter part of an article written by John Fischer in 1968, entitled "Open Letter to the Next President"

Dear Mr. { McCarthy
             Nixon
             Humphrey
             Rockefeller } as the case may be:

. . . .

What this might save is hard to guess, but throughout your term of office it might well run to a hundred billion. Moreover, if we and the Russians stop glaring at each other,* both of us could save additional billions we are now wasting on prestige projects. For example, the race to the moon. No doubt it would be interesting to see what is up there someday—but if the Russians get the first peek, what of it? And if our own space buffs can't contain their curiosity for a few decades, let them go raise the money for their own moon shot, from the Ford Foundation or Howard Hughes or somebody. I can't think of a single reason why the taxpayers should get stuck for it.[2]

*This doesn't mean that we should close our eyes, since there is no evidence that the Kremlin is about to abandon the classic goals of Marxism-Leninism. But there is a lot of difference between a glare and a state of calm, attentive watchfulness.

The title of John Fischer's regular column, "The Easy Chair," signals his aim: to write in a relaxed style about the things friends might discuss comfortably in their favorite chairs.

That paragraph and its conversational footnote is an example of an informal and casual style, but notice how carefully it was constructed. The transition to the previous paragraph is there, but casually expressed, "What this might save." The "this" refers to recommendations Fischer made in the previous paragraph about cutting down appropriations. A colloquial phrase like "hard to guess" makes the passage sound like one neighbor's chatting with another as he fixes his car or paints the porch. Another example of casual talk—"might well run to a hundred billion"—sounds general, but indicates the kind of information Fischer probably does have. "Moreover" is an example of a formal word from rhetoric books, but he follows it quickly with "if we and the Russians stop glaring at one another," language appropriate for angry football teams, not the mightiest of nations.

Fischer varies sentence structure, too: "For example, the race to the moon," a sentence fragment, typical of speech. Notice the antiheroic way of putting man's great adventure, "No doubt it would be interesting to see what is up there sometime," as if he spoke about the attic. He calls the thrilling sight of all time "the first peek," in the language of children looking at a birthday present, and calls the space scientists "space buffs." This style communicates an idea central to this article. Fischer does not say it is childish to be pouring money into space travel, but he implies as much by the lilt of, "And if . . . let them go raise the money for their own moon shot," which sounds like, "let them go get the money for their own game of marbles." The "or somebody" is casual, but it suggests as well that Fischer knows it won't be so easy to get that amount of money.

That last sentence could have been said in much more formal fashion. Fischer wrote, "I can't think of a single reason why the taxpayers should get stuck for it." He could have written in formal style, "It is exceedingly difficult to comprehend why the burden for this unnecessary venture should be placed upon individual taxpay-· ers," but that would not be the speech of neighbor talking to neighbor, as commonly considered anyway. Fischer's "get stuck for it" is about as slangy as his articles ever get. The result of his slang is that a reader feels that Fischer is an ordinary man in touch with the things that matter to ordinary men. Still, if one watches his writing rather closely over a period of years, it becomes clear that this colloquial method permits him to pass on information that is not usually considered part of light reading. He alternates casual word choice with impressive amounts of information and provocative insights, but the casual style is the art concealing art which permits the reader to read away, thinking the article is all entertainment. Of course, it is entertaining, often amusing, almost always thought-provoking. Consider the footnote. What part of it is stated simply, unpretentiously? What part indicates to you that the modest style is used by an informed writer?

As a fairly sharp contrast to Fischer's paragraph, consider this one from John Kenneth Galbraith's article "The Day Khrushchev Visited the Establishment." Galbraith's article shows a scene in which American representatives of the so-called Establishment "ask" Khrushchev questions and make speeches while doing so. Galbraith calls this exhausting process, " 'I would like to tell you something,' they asked."

The next question I subsequently estimated at twenty minutes—but this could have been an impression. It was put—perhaps one could better say composed—by the Chairman of the Radio Corporation of America, General David Sarnoff himself. Mr. Sarnoff's manner (at least to Khrushchev) could best be described as imperial. He made it clear at the outset that no disagreement would be tolerated. He began with a detailed outline of the free American system of broadcasting. He continued with a warm tribute to its freedom—and some statistics on the number of stations currently on the air. This question was punctuated by some pounding of the Sarnoff breast. No mention was made of commercials. The question was itself a commercial. The General then depicted the refined and varied blessings that would accrue were Russia to adopt a similar system employing a maximum of American programming. When he finished there was silence—a total solemn silence. On this question Khrushchev rose to the greatest heights of the meeting, perhaps indeed of the entire visit. After a general word or two he said, "Things have changed in Minsk since you were a boy."[3]

The style contributes to the subject in Galbraith's paragraph, partly because the subject is pretentiousness being reduced by simplicity. And Khrushchev's simple speech, which shows he knows boastful pretensions when he sees them, contrasts nicely with Galbraith's own formality. Galbraith, in fact, makes a joke of his own formality: "The next question I subsequently estimated at twenty minutes—but [he adds politely] this could have been an impression." But what a long impression. The fun here is partly in the formality of "subsequently estimated," because the reader translates that into an imaginative picture of Galbraith saying to himself later, "How long *did* that 'question' take?"

Galbraith is used to speaking with care and to having people listen to him with attention, as his, "It was put—perhaps one could better say composed" indicates. He is used to having his audiences note the difference between "putting" a question and "composing" one. A simple man "puts" a question; a pretentious man "composes" one. A composed question will be elaborate, reflecting glory on the composer. A "put" question will just get it said, if possible. But Galbraith refrains from calling General Sarnoff pompous. He says, "Mr. Sarnoff's manner . . . could best be described as imperial." The full weight of the sentence falls on "imperial" at the end of the sentence after the author kept us in suspense by "could best be described."

The Galbraith manner, or style, is that of a conscious wit who chooses his words with care and knows his audience knows it. Fischer clearly chooses his words with care, but he uses art to conceal that he does, because it suits him to develop the manner of the ordinary intelligent man talking to friends. Even a reader who is not in his confidence can see that his choice of style was judicious for his purpose. Fischer's style permits concentration on his content, but Galbraith's style draws attention to itself and becomes a source of wit. In this sentence, through a formal style Galbraith makes fun of what Sarnoff said. "The General then depicted the refined and varied blessings that would accrue were Russia to adopt a similar system employing a maximum of American programming." Sarnoff is giving the hard sell, but "refined and varied blessing" disguises with elegance all that Sarnoff says Russia would get from American methods. "Accrue," rare in casual speech, is a formal verb meaning "to grow as a natural result." Here, Sarnoff may be talking of money pouring in, but Galbraith speaks of "refined and varied blessings that would accrue."

Part of Galbraith's fun is that retelling the event in his formal speech disguises, but only thinly, the rather crass and pushing quality of the whole event: important men who were asking "questions" that served their own interests and a guest who was also serving his own interests. The civilized quality of Galbraith's formal speech underlines, by contrast, the not-so-civilized nature of the high-level diplomatic event. His formal style in this passage is, in short, a prime source of his wit.

What Is a General Characteristic of the Formal Style?

The formal style is not always, or even usually, used for wit. Probably its most basic element, aside from its nonconversational level of word choice, is its balancing of sentence elements—for clarity, not wit. The following passage is taken from Henry James's scenario for *The Ambassadors,* which he sent to magazine editors before he had written the novel. In this passage he describes Lambert Strether, the central figure of the novel:

He is an American, of the present hour and of sufficiently typical New England origin, who has, at the point of his career that he has reached, the consciousness of a good deal of prolonged effort and tension, the memory of a good many earnest and anxious experiments—professional, practical, intellectual, moral, personal—to look back upon, without, for himself, any very proportionate sense of acknowledged or achieved success. However, he is, in the rather provincial, the somewhat contracted world in which he lives, a highly esteemed figure and influence. Educated, with excellent gifts, intelligent, having passed, for the most part, as exceptionally "clever," he has had a life by no means wasted, but not happily concentrated; and rather makes on himself the impression of having come in for many of the drawbacks, even perhaps for [a] little of the discredit, of an incoherent existence, without, unfortunately, any of the accompanying entertainment or "fun." He feels tired, in other words, without having a great deal to show for it; disenchanted without having known any great enchantments, enchanters, or, above all, enchantresses; and even before the action in which he is engaged launches him, is vaguely haunted by the feeling of what he has missed, though this is a quantity, and a quality, that he would be rather at a loss to name.[4]

The first quality in this passage that may strike you is the length of the individual sentences. It is difficult to write a long sentence and keep its meaning clear. You may notice that within these long sentences there are many phrases of different lengths, and there are clauses containing parallel phrases like "who has . . . the consciousness of . . . the memory of. . . ." These balanced sentence elements hold the meaning clear but require attention to the very end of the sentence. Read this passage aloud, trying to vary the rise and fall of your intonation to make the reading clear to a listener.

Certain parts of the passage are unfamiliar. Try to focus on them to discover why a section is unclear. Often it helps to translate a hard part into your own words entirely. With that method, you can see what you do not understand and often work it out. The use of "experiments" seems odd. James uses the word in a broad sense, meaning, not experiments in a laboratory, but the cautious testing, trying out that people do in living. Can you think of some typical examples of experiments in "professional, practical, intellectual, moral, personal" realms? However, Strether is "a highly esteemed figure and influence." Again the phrasing is unfamiliar, but the idea is quite recognizable. We might say he was "an influential figure," but that phrase implies ambition and wealth, which is not at all James's meaning here. James is succinct in saying, "he has had a life by no means wasted, but not happily concentrated. . . ." That is a difficult idea to express. We might say something like: Strether had not focused his energies or worked long enough at one thing to his own satisfaction. The word "clever" is in quotation marks in James's passage because he refers to a term used in sophisticated conversation of that day as some people today might put quotes around "with it," in "He was considered by his peers to be 'with it.' " In twenty years, "with it" will have to be explained, as "clever" has to be interpreted for us. James's phrase, "having passed, for the most part, as exceptionally 'clever,' " might be translated: Strether was considered by most people, for most of his life, as bright, sophisticated—one who was witty and amusing at a party. To paraphrase the next-to-last sentence: Strether feels that he has experienced the disadvantages and perhaps even the disapproval that accompanies an aimless life without having had its pleasures. Simplifying the gist of the passage in this way, the reader can examine James's method more closely.

James's last sentence sums up the previous sentences well. His "in other words" warns the reader to take note of an approaching summary. The essential balance of the last sentence is based on the two things that Strether "feels" and the one thing he "is."

He feels
    tired, in other words,
        without having a great deal to show for it;
    disenchanted
        without having known any great enchantments,
            enchanters, or, above all, enchantresses;
    and even
        before the action in which he is engaged
            launches him,
is vaguely haunted
    by the feeling
        of what he has missed,
            though this is a quantity, and a quality,
                that he would be rather at a loss to name.

Such a general graph gives a visual picture of the three elements upon which all the other qualifying phrases and clauses depend. The formal rhetorical structure, then, is not used in this example for wit or humor, but merely to clarify all the ideas through subordination and parallelism, to keep their logical relationship clear to the reader.

The use of that balancing technique is even more clear in the next passage, taken from John Henry Cardinal Newman's *The Idea of a University:*

> Nor indeed am I supposing that there is any great danger, at least in this day, of overeducation; the danger is on the other side. I will tell you, Gentlemen, what has been the practical error of the last twenty years—not to load the memory of the student with a mass of undigested knowledge, but to force upon him so much that he has rejected all. It has been the error of distracting and enfeebling the mind by an unmeaning profusion of subjects; of implying that a smattering in a dozen branches of study is not shallowness, which it really is, but enlargement, which it is not; of considering an acquaintance with the learned names of things and persons, and the possession of clever duodecimos, and attendance on eloquent lecturers, and membership with scientific institutions, and the sight of the experiments of a platform and the specimens of a museum, that all this was not dissipation of mind, but progress. All things now are to be learned at once, not first one thing, then another, not one well, but many badly. Learning is to be without exertion, without attention, without toil; without grounding, without advance, without finishing. There is to be nothing individual in it; and this, forsooth, is the wonder of the age. What the steam engine does with matter, the printing press is to do with mind; it is to act mechanically, and the population is to be passively, almost unconsciously enlightened by the mere multiplication and dissemination of volumes.[5]

Newman's clear emphatic prose may not express your own opinion, but there is no mistaking his. Read it over to see the balance of its elements. Not to do this—but to do that. "It has been the error of distracting and enfeebling . . . ," of implying that X is not Y, which it really is, but Z which it is not. Perhaps the best indicators of formal prose are precision of diction and the balance of sentence elements, the parallel of forms like "of distracting and enfeebling . . . of implying" with repetitions and contrasts. "All things now are to be learned at once, not first one thing, then another, not one well, but many badly." Formal prose does not mean dull, muddied, boring prose, and it can be highly distinctive as well as controversial.

There are many, many other places on that long spectrum of style, from Fischer's casual, conversational style used in "The Easy Chair" to Newman's strongly balanced sentences and formal prose, shown in *The Idea of the University*. And no author is limited to one style. Fischer often uses balanced rhetorical elements in more formal pieces, and Newman writes a beautifully polished sinuous line when he chooses. But briefly, to illustrate some different uses of style, consider these examples. There is a slangy style that can catch a moment:

> "Naw, I go first," I said. "It's my old lady. If I ain't cool enough to take care of her, I ain't cool enough to have her."
> The music was way out and the well-timed beat of hundreds of feet made a *chevere* noise on the wooden floor of the Palladium. I nodded to Louie and made my way through the twisting mambo-mad people. The cat had just swung Trina out again with the intention of slamming her into him again when I stepped in between them and snatched her cool, without losing a dance step, and kept dancing with her. The cat looked like a fool and jumped stink. "Hey, man, whatcha putting down?" he said angrily. "Can't you see I'm dancing with the broad?"
> I stopped dancing and didn't even look at the cat. I took Trina by the hand and walked off the dance floor.
> "It's not my fault, Piri," she said.[6]

If you underline the cool talk in that passage, you will see that it is not as large a proportion of the language as you think. Just a few words, like "ain't" "cool" "cat," suggest that the whole passage is as jazzy as the writer intended.

The simplicity and restraint of style in a passage by another author suggests that the speaker is a man in control of himself:

> Yesterday I lost my license.
> To a professional steeplechase jockey, losing his license and being warned off Newmarket Heath is like being chucked off the medical register, only more so.
> Barred from race riding, barred from race courses. Barred, moreover, from racing stables. Which poses me quite a problem, as I live in one.
> No livelihood and maybe no home.
> Last night was a right so-and-so, and I prefer to forget those grisly sleepless hours. Shock and bewilderment, the feeling that

it couldn't have happened, it was all a mistake. . . . This lasted until after midnight. And at least the disbelieving stage had had some built-in comfort. The full thudding realization which followed had none at all. My life was lying around like untidy bits of a smashed teacup, and I was altogether out of glue and rivets.[7]

The restraint in content (no hysterics or shouts of rage and revenge) is expressed through restraint in style (no ornaments, transitions, extra words). He doesn't even say, *I have been* "barred from race riding. . . ." The writer uses sentence fragments, like staccato speech, to suggest jumping thoughts. Word choice and punctuation express two basic ideas: that the speaker has experienced a disaster and that he is a strong, determined man not easily crushed. The reader wants to know, of course, how such a disaster could have happened to this cool-headed hero—an excellent beginning for this mystery novel.

In another passage, the style suggests tedium, the cliché-ridden mind of a boring railroad companion:

> Mrs. Hitchcock said neither was she. She told him she had been a Miss Weatherman before she married and that she was going to Florida to visit her married daughter, Sarah Lucile. She said it seemed like she had never had time to take a trip that far off. The way things happened, one thing after another, it seemed like time went by so fast you couldn't tell if you were young or old.
> He thought he could tell her she was old if she asked him. He stopped listening to her after a while.[8]

The author's style is chosen to portray dullness. She does not give Mrs. Hitchcock's dull words directly: "Neither am I. I was a Miss Weatherman before I married. I am going to Florida to visit my married daughter, Sarah Lucile." That would be boring, but not as deadly as the author's use of indirect discourse makes it. (She said that . . .)

Try using indirect discourse yourself, and watch the change from, for example, the excitement of, "Help me! I've fallen off the fire escape and think I've broken my arm," to, "He cried out for help. He said that he had fallen off the fire escape and thought he had broken his arm." Flannery O'Connor chose to subtract excitement and even interest from poor Mrs. Hitchcock's boring remarks.

Put these in indirect discourse:

- The fire has reached the haystack. You've got to come off with me. Jump into the wagon.
- I tell you the horse is drugged. You can't take a chance on riding a drugged horse in a steeplechase.
- My sheets and towels are whiter than white because I use Fluffo-White with that built-in lemon-downy freshness.

The choice of words, the style of a passage, helps the writer to express his meaning, as Dick Francis expressed character through word choice and sentence fragments and Flannery O'Connor suggested Mrs. Hitchcock's boring mind through indirect discourse. A book can have many different styles, from racy through gentle, slangy and "with it" through formal or poetic, or mixtures of all of these.

How Does the Young Writer Develop His Own Style?

That question is misleading. First, it implies that there is or should be one style for each person. As there is no one style of dress or speech for all occasions, there is no one style of writing that is always appropriate. Further, if there were one style for any occasion, the question would mean, "Tell me the style appropriate to my identity so I can use it at all times." That answer cannot be supplied by anyone but oneself, and the variability and range of each person's nature would quite properly resist any one style for all seasons. But, style is not, in fact, chosen to fit the personality, but primarily to suit the purpose, and part of the author's purpose is to have a certain effect on a certain audience. It is like the clothing selected for rough work or for athletics, for a church service or for a wedding. Which kinds of words should be used for a letter of complaint to the school newspaper, a letter of resignation, a letter of apology, a letter of condolence? "What style is right for this purpose?" is a better question than "How do I develop my own style?"

Expect to use many different styles, depending on your purpose and audience; letters written home, to a friend, to a newspaper, to an unknown cousin might each have a different style. "Had a real great time at the movies" written to a friend might turn into "My friends and I went to an interesting movie last night" written to a strict uncle. There are many words for each word, and there are idioms, slang, and in-group ways of passing on the same news: went to the movies. This variety of possibilities is what is meant by varieties of styles. Every person's selection depends on his purpose at a particular moment.

The first goal of the developing writer and the ultimate goal of any writer is the same: to develop a broad-ranging, flexible vocabulary and a sensitivity to language that permits him to express accurately his full range of attitudes, feelings, and ideas—in short to be able to say what he means. But consider your own position; it is like any other writer's. At first all you may "mean" is to express an idea or a feeling. But later it is not enough to express "it" (whatever it is) to your own satisfaction. You will wish someone else to view the matter as you do yourself. Sometimes this results in an essay of persuasion written as a "Letter to the Editor" and sometimes in a love poem, but the awareness of the audience in both cases has affected the word choice or the style.

How Does Style Apply to Student Writing?

Style applies to student writing as it does to any other: the words chosen need to be appropriate to the audience and to your purpose. If you speak as one intelligent being to another, basing your discussion on logic and reasoning, your language will be as clear and objective, as rational and as well supported by illustrations as you can make it. If you are writing to stir the emotions, you might invoke emotional clichés and pitch your discourse at that emotional level. If you are writing an essay on what you have seen and experienced—the changes that have come to your city or home town in recent years, for example—you are writing as a kind of expert. You know what has happened to your family better than anyone in your audience, perhaps, excluding your own family. Your tone can be assured, definite; it expresses your actual relation to that subject. If you are writing on Mark Twain, having read one book and two stories, you cannot pose as an expert. Although you may still say firmly what you see in his writing, you would avoid sweeping generalizations about all of his writing, as if you had read it all.

tone

What Is Tone?

Tone is the emotional atmosphere, the feeling expressed through the words chosen and the vocal intonation.

> Is this your best work? It is hardly my idea of freshman work.

In speech, a scathing, bitter tone is expressed through vocal intonation as well as words.

> Father settled himself in his chair, picked up his fork, tucked his napkin under his shirt collar saying, "My favorite pie."

Comfort, contentment, pleasure may be in father's tone and in his gestures, but words alone can express tone. Try to hear the rousing tone of this speech from *Henry V,* encouraging men to battle in the old heroic style:

He that cutlives this day and comes safe home
Will stand a tip-toe when this day is named. . . .
We few, we happy few, we band of brothers.
For he to-day that sheds his blood with me
Shall be my brother. . . .

And gentlemen in England now a-bed
Shall think themselves accurs'd they were not here,
And hold their manhoods cheap whiles any speaks
That fought with us upon Saint Crispin's Day.[9]

Henry V was asking men to go, perhaps, to death with him, but his patriotic words and their rousing tone were persuasive as Shakespeare rendered it. What is the tone of this passage?

We are not fighting for the right to be like you. We respect ourselves too much for that. When we fight for freedom, we mean freedom for us to be black, or brown, and you to be white and yet live together in a free and equal society. This is the only way that integration can mean dignity for both of us.

I, for one, am growing weary of those well-meaning white liberals who are forever telling me they don't know what color I am. The very fact that they single me out at the cocktail party and gratuitously make me the beneficiary of their blessed assurances gives the lie to their pronouncements.

My fight is not *for* racial sameness, but for racial equality and *against* racial prejudice and discrimination. I work for the day when my people will be free of the racist pressures to be *white like you;* a day when "good hair" and "high yaller" and bleaching cream and hair-straighteners will be obsolete.[10]

The tone is urgent, insistent, close to exasperation, that of an honest man speaking a plain style. The simple style that seems to express integrity becomes pompous only once, at the moment the author mocks those who single him out at cocktail parties and "gratuitously make [him] the beneficiary of their blessed assurances. . . ." Those elaborate words, so unlike the simplicity of the rest of the language quoted, mock the intellectual pretentions of the liberals who may speak well but who do not see that their actions prove that they do think of his color. The tone of the pompous phrase is contemptuous and scornful.

Vroooooom . . . the Autopub is very racy . . . a Licorice Kandy Kolored Chrome Flake Streamline Monster Baby in the lower chassis of the General Motors Building—a gas from Longchamps.

It is Manhattan's freshest must. Absolutely obligatory for kids and visiting homefolks. Clearly, a fortune has been spent to create an autobug's fantasy: all those upside-down racing cars and carburetors and muffler mockups, the racing helmet fixtures, the bucket seats, the tufted vicuña colored leatherette of the Eldorado Pullman car . . . the bus boys in Getty overalls . . . the unpretentious Loreleis in hot pants . . . what prepubescent under 60 could possibly resist?[11]

This breezy, in-group tone probably is the best one to use to describe a restaurant in New York City where the specialty does not appear to be food, but its setting—a car buff's heaven. Gael Greene imitates Tom Wolfe's title, *The Kandy-Kolored Tangerine-Flake Streamline Baby,* and its surrealistic incoherence. She probably mocks herself in calling the restaurant "Manhattan's freshest must." A "must" is one of the tiredest clichés in a reviewer's vocabulary. Look up "prepubescent" before you decide that she thinks the restaurant is great. Two of her later sentences suggest another view: "But mostly the food is drearily mediocre and consistently tepid: the sliced steak is tough but tasty. . . . The giant omelette must have been pre-cast." The tone of the passage is assured, sophisticated, rather disdainful, but trying to be fair: "There are some pleasant touches . . . ." The only way to bring most people to read about food is to have a remarkable style that brings fun to thoughts of "fresh-grated horseradish" and "mashed apricots."[12] The topic is, from a certain perspective, absurd, but style can make even mashed apricots interesting.

Then there is the kind of thing known as "time style":

The first hot breath of summer is upon the land, and with it has come a perennially deepening dementia that turns otherwise lucid adults into drooling, lip-smacking lunatics, children into chocolate-mustachioed gluttons and family dogs into insatiable beggars. This year, more than ever before, they all scream for ice cream.
Americans have always been afflicted with ice-creamania. Their per capita consumption, currently [is] at 30 pints a year. . . . Though the invention of ice cream is usually credited to the Emperor Nero, it was the U.S. that gave mankind the ice-cream cone and the soda. Now there are signs of a fundamental shift in the frozen foundations of the Republic: Americans are beginning to turn a cold shoulder to the three pillars of their forefathers' frigid faith—chocolate, strawberry and vanilla—and flocking to

flagrantly concupiscent flavors like Passion Fruit, Kumquat, Papaya, Sparkling Burgundy and Brandy Alexander.[13]

This is time style, a particular brand of hyperbolical journalese meant to make it pleasant to read about business in the Marketing Section. "Leading the gallop to gloppiness in Baskin-Robbins, a California-based franchise chain with $52 million in annual sales" is a typical beginning, with an alliterative phrase (one that repeats initial consonants like *g*)—"gallop to gloppiness"—followed by an overpacked mound of facts and adjectives. Puns, like "unslurpassed," and alliterating adjectives and nouns, like "ice-cream cravers can commit caloric immolation," call attention to the verbal facility and general cuteness. The point of the article is to tell about Baskin-Robbins, who "began merchandising mirth in 1949," but either embarrassed to be discussing the subject or convinced that no one has the mind to read about the business without psychedelic verbiage, the writer's filigree work calls attention to itself. The writer may suppose the reader will miss the condescending tone within the humor. He would not be sporting on the high wires if he thought his readers could bear Baskin-Robbins without help.

Tone is a direct result of style, the words chosen. It is impossible to write in no-tone, as it is impossible to write or dress in no-style. As style can be casual, formal, fashionable, conventional, messy, or haphazard, for example, tone may be monotonous, or moderate, or quiet, but the words carry something, some emotional atmosphere from flat or objective to angry or frivolous. Tone is, in this sense, the author's attitude toward his subject coming through his words.

How Is Tone Expressed?

Even when it is clear what tone is, it may not be clear at first how tone, the author's attitude toward the subject, is communicated to the reader. Whether or not he is conscious of it, the author's emotional attitude toward himself, his audience, and his subject is conveyed by: the words chosen, their order of expression (syntax), the connotations of words as well as their denotation, the use of metaphors and similes, and the kinds of comparisons chosen. All of these together create the author's style in a passage, and through his style, his tone is expressed. Although they all work dynamically within one context, each is interesting to consider separately for a moment, but it is not easy or even sensible to separate them for long.

What Are Connotation and Denotation, and How Do They Work to Express Tone?

A word's denotation is its dictionary meaning, and its connotation is the cluster of emotional associations that comes to be attached to the word in addition to its denotation. The word "lamp" for instance is well known. A child might point out a lamp in a furniture store. He knows that the sound "lamp" denotes or signifies any one of the varieties of electrical objects with light bulbs and shades. Some lamps are for students at their desks, some hang down from the ceiling, some stand on white iron poles, and so on. The connotation of the sound "lamp" might be quite different to different people. To a child afraid of the dark, it might suggest calmness and his mother sewing nearby. To others, it might have religious associations connected with lamps in church or patriotic associations connected with the Statue of Liberty. It might be associated with Florence Nightingale, who was known as the Lady of the Lamp, or Diogenes, who is said to have carried a lantern in his search for an honest man. All the uses of a word that a person has read, seen, heard, or thought, gather in the mind. The word then has emotional meaning beyond its dictionary definition or denotation. Clever use of words can draw upon some part of this reservoir of connotative suggestion.

"Darkness" has a simple denotation. It refers to somber shades or the absence of light, but the connotation of the word "darkness" is vast. It may be associated with a peaceful time when the house is quiet, or with a sinister, threatening time of fear, probably grounded in man's primitive fear of the dark. In literature it has been associated with ignorance and evil. An individual will have many or few associations with a word, depending on his actual experience and his imaginative experience through reading, listening, and films. One person's experience may, of course, be thinner than another person's in one respect, but richer in another, yet the writer writes for everyone who cares to read his work. He may take pains to communicate with a great range of his audience, or he may choose to ignore those who cannot grasp his personal references. Through his use of a word, his syntax and references, a writer can make clear his selection of the meanings to be associated with the word.

Although each person's experience is unique, still we share so much that writers can choose words that work upon us through their connotations. The writer also can build up his own meaning in his own context so that the reader will rule out one set of connotations and accept only those the writer emphasizes. In *Heart of Darkness,* Joseph Conrad begins by using the heart of darkness to refer to the center of the African Congo, but finally the heart of darkness is described as within man, even the so-called cultivated, idealistic man that Mr. Kurtz was before he went to the Congo and became corrupted by his lusts for power and ivory. When the narrator of the novel hears about certain ceremonies "used when approaching Mr. Kurtz," he protests. He refuses to hear them described, fearing that he would be "transported into some lightless region of subtle horrors, where pure, uncomplicated savagery was a positive relief, being something that has a right to exist—obviously—in the sunshine."[14] Savagery, he thinks, then, compared to Kurtz's depravity, should exist in the sunshine. But later, the narrator thinks that Kurtz had dared, at least, to look into the darkness of man's heart:

> Since I had peeped over the edge myself, I understand better
> the meaning of his stare, that could not see the flame of the candle,
> but was wide enough to embrace the whole universe, piercing
> enough to penetrate all the hearts that beat in the darkness. He
> had summed up—he had judged. "The horror!"[15]

There is much more that could be said about tone and Conrad's evocation of atmosphere, but what is important here is that the single word "darkness," which has a simple denotation that any child knows, is extended further and further by Conrad's use of it, until other connotations of darkness are excluded and the reader follows only Conrad's multiple meanings. Still, the reader is moved by the emotional connotations of darkness: the darkness of the primitive and the primitive within men and each man, the darkness of the unknown, of the unknowable, of the obscure, as well as the darkness of the sinister and the evil that Conrad finds in the heart of man. In the novel, peace, tranquility, and the erotic are almost entirely ruled out of Conrad's associations with darkness.

Despite the uniqueness of human experience, we share much,

both in terms of direct and imagined experience, through our heritage of songs and stories. Writers can draw upon this shared experience within a certain range, provided their own contexts are clear. The color green has many associations for most people. Like darkness, it is intimately a part of everyone's experience, excluding only those who live in a land of continual snow and ice or those who cannot see color. It is a part of religious awareness that goes back to man's earliest vegetation myths and the wonder of the land's rebirth in the spring. Green has been a symbol of hope, of jealousy, of the supernatural, of youth. Yet in "Fern Hill," Dylan Thomas draws upon this rich reservoir of connotation for his own purposes in his own way. At the end of this exquisite lyric, after so many associations of green with joy, and youth, and intensity of life, the poet turns and pulls against these connotations in his last two lines, saying, "Time held me green and dying. / Though I sang in my chains like the sea." While he was young (green), he was still in time's power, and though young, he was still dying, yet singing as the sea does, locked as it is in the same inevitable fashion by the land. The shock of "green and dying" is that contradicting pull of opposites, because green is rarely associated with death.

The connotative powers of words are inexhaustible, because human experience and its variety is inexhaustible. Still, despite this variety, advertisers can count on the reactions of most people to words like "new," "modern," "fashionable," "elegant," "youthful" to exploit them to sell instant coffee or cars. "Youthful" can be associated with a car, and "elegant" can sell shoes. "Old" will sell wine, Scotch, antiques, some houses; but the connotation of "new" seems to be much more invigorating. "Move up to Unigrab. Drive the prestige car." Such slogans play upon the audience's aspirations to "move up" to something "above" wherever they are, their desire to have "prestige," or respect from others. The connotation of words, not their denotation, sells carbonated drinks. Some bottled drinks are associated with youth, "the Burpsie generation" swingers who "have a lot to live."

Many products are sold through the snobbish connotations of the words used in their advertisements. Consider any group of advertisements closely. Observe their pictures and study the texts that accompany them. If the text said the absolute truth, it might read something like this:

This is a pretty good Scotch; that is, it tastes fairly good to those who like Scotch, but it doesn't have the smoky taste that some people prefer. If you drink moderately, it may relax you before dinner. It is not wise to drink too much of this though, because there is something in it that gives some people heartburn.

We made it in the ordinary kind of wooden vat and brewed it for five years, as is pretty usual.

Instead, using the power of connotations the text reads something like this:

Here is the drink for men of decision, men who know quality, the drink for the quiet hours [picture of elegant couple on balcony overlooking lights of the city and linked lights of the George Washington Bridge] when responsible men relax after the day's challenge.

To men like these we offer our vintage Scotch, brewed lovingly by the Brainton Family's secret formula, to just that perfect touch of rich lightness enjoyed by sophisticated palates.

In this parody, the text is typically uninformative: no facts, but plenty of suggestion. Snob appeal is patent; this is no picture of two gray-haired women. Those who enjoy the drink are associated with "men of decision," that is, men who make decisions. Since an ordinary decision is usually called "making up your mind," or "a choice," this is an important choice—hence "decision." Those who make decisions are powerful people, not ordinary clucks like you and me. But if we wish to be considered powerful, we will of course, drink Brainton's Scotch. (The name is typically Anglo-Saxon.)

The advertiser knows that the ordinary man wants to convince himself that he is like the man in the Brainton Scotch ad: brainy (makes decisions), powerful, handsome, sophisticated (with beautiful woman on balcony overlooking most sophisticated city in the world)—a man who meets "challenges" every day and needs to rest and relax after a difficult day of "tensions." The Scotch is called "vintage," a rich, wonderful word suggesting the aging ripeness of wine. Probably every brewer has his own method, but to call it a "secret formula" elevates it far above a "recipe," which any cook can have. A favorite trick of copywriters is to set two adjectives against one another like rich/lightness. If a drink is rich, it is not usually light, and vice versa; but if the copywriter uses both words, he can have it both ways and appeal to everyone. The far-out hyperbole, like "sophisticated palate," is absurd but often used. It makes as much sense as calling a nose "intuitive," but we come to swallow such usage, and do not even notice it going down.

An interesting experiment in connotations is to take one word and vary it as often as you can according to shifts in connotation. Take a word that refers to instructions on how to make something: "directions" or "instructions." For this there is also "recipe" and "formula." "Recipe" is the modest word women use to refer to the "instructions" they follow in the kitchen. "Formula" suggests scientists in the laboratory or mathematicians at a blackboard. For another example, if you put "making up one's mind" on a scale of ascending importance or power, it might go like this:

> to deem
> to judge
> to determine
> to decide
> to choose
> to make up your mind

In the typical language of conventional hierarchy: a child makes up his mind, a woman chooses, and a man decides. (That patriarchal hierarchy is not to be perpetuated mindlessly, but to be understood as you increase in sensitivity to the way words commonly are used.)

Take a verb like "to wish" and range it along a scale of increasing determination. It might go this way: "wish," "would like," "request," "want," "insist," "demand." The shock of revolutionary speech is that it maintains the shriek level from the beginning. It does not work up the ladder from "would like" to "demand."

Try moving up a scale of intensity, using these words as starters: "pleasant," "colorful," "old," "attractive," "wrong," "follow," "dislike," "agree."

What Does Context Have to Do with Tone?

Everything. The context determines the connotation of the word that the writer is using. Words can have any number of meanings and connotative suggestions. The word "apple" can refer to the particular fruit on the kitchen table or to the one that Eve is said to have eaten. The context (that passage in which the word was found) primarily determines which of all the possible meanings of "apple" will be invoked. A recent ad for *Time* magazine used a large, red, firm-looking apple with a bite out of it, and a word like "tempting" as its caption. The ad exploited for humor the temptation of the Garden of Eden. The reader was being tempted to subscribe to *Time* by the low rates offered. So soundly embedded in the Western tradition is the Garden of Eden story that "apple," "bite," and "tempting" could carry the message, and when linked to the new subject, it could be amusing. In another context, however—for example, a healthy, bright-eyed child sitting on a rock and biting an apple, while watching her friends climbing a tree and shaking down apples—allusions to Eve and Eden would have no place.

Temporal context affects tone, too. Since the rise in drug use, some words have gained new connotations—words like "pipe," "grass," "rush," "speed," "pop"; while words like "swastika," "setting sun," "drill," "radar," "search light," and even "concentration camp" have tended to lose their power to arouse war-time associations. Fearing the unwanted pun, a writer probably would not call his book *Rush to Judgment* now, or *The Grass Harp.* But language changes rapidly, and in another five years, other words that are now fairly uncommunicative emotionally, like "clothes line," "beagle," or "curbstone," may attain unexpected connotations, and the puns on "grass" may fade out of memory.

What Do Metaphors and Similes Have to Do with Tone?

Essentially, metaphors and similes are ways to bring unlike objects, ideas, or qualities together—not precisely to compare them, but to describe one term through the characteristics of the other. "She is a pill" is a metaphor. It is not literally true that the lady is a pill, but she does, unfortunately, have certain characteristics of the typical pill. She is bitter, unpleasant; she makes no attempt to please. The "is" makes the device called a metaphor. A simile uses "like" or "as" "He is like a runaway train." The speed, lack of direction of the train out of control are evoked to suggest this person's characteristics. A metaphor or simile that is apt can sustain the writer's meaning, even clarify it, by carrying out the main ideas and suggesting other qualities, usually emotional, as well. If comparisons are not apt, they can shift the sense of a passage, confuse it, or dislocate its tone.

In George Orwell's *1984* there is, in the early part of the novel, a shocking description of one of the daily routines, "Two Minutes Hate," in the lives of the characters. Two minutes are spent regularly, at a certain time each day, in rage at the figure that appears on the telescreen. These moments of screaming are meant to provide a release through which hate may be expressed and yet directed constructively—that is, according to the government's wishes. The narrator says, "And yet the rage that one felt was an abstract, undirected emotion which could be switched from one object to another like the flame of a blowlamp."[16] As a blowlamp, or blowtorch to Americans, may be aimed at an object, shoot flames at it, and be turned swiftly to a new spot, so the rage worked up in Two Minutes Hate could be switched from object to object—from Goldstein, the public enemy of Two Minutes Hate, to another character in the novel. The purity of this undirected but directable rage is almost explained by the simile. Further, the flame imagery carries out the notion of the heat or the intensity of rage. But suppose Orwell had written, instead of "like the flame of a blowlamp," "like the spurt of a hose"? A hose can switch from object to object; that aspect of his comparison would be retained. But the heat generated by the blowlamp comparison, which works to express rage well, would be counteracted by the idea of water, which quenches fire and heat. The two qualities of Orwell's image—directability and heat—are not both carried out by the "spurt of the hose" comparison. Suppose he had written "like turning on an electric light switch." Orwell's meaning then would be garbled, because a light switch goes off and on and Orwell speaks of turning from object to object.

If the writer can avoid the comparison that is a cliché (fresh as paint, smooth as silk), and if he can manage to select a metaphor or simile that supports the meaning of his sentence and its subjective qualities as well, imagery can be enormously helpful. In *1984* Orwell describes the hero, Winston Smith, receiving a precious piece of black market chocolate. Orwell seems to bring his camera in to take a close-up of the piece of chocolate:

Even before he had taken it he knew by the smell that it was very unusual chocolate. It was dark and shiny, and was wrapped in silver paper. Chocolate normally was dull-brown crumbly stuff that tasted, as nearly as one could describe it, like the smoke of a rubbish fire. But at some time or another he had tasted chocolate like the piece she had given him.[17]

Orwell engages smell, sight, touch, taste indirectly and simply. The simile, when it appears, is almost unnoticed, but it carries the sense impressions further and serves to express an emotional quality, too. If Orwell had compared the taste to the smoke of burning plastic, he might have conveyed the nastiness of the odor, but the suggestion of burning "rubbish" is worse. Rubbish is composed of old, broken, and abandoned objects, but plastic suggests cheap, new things. In addition to an acrid nastiness, "the smoke of a rubbish fire" suggests disappointment and depression, far from the expectations that the black market chocolate arouses in Winston Smith. Orwell, then, used the simile to support his central meaning and to suggest background, subjective qualities as well.

"To talk to him was like listening to the tinkling of a worn-out musical box."[18] How easily Orwell suggests Mr. Charrington's age, fragility, civilization, delicacy, and fastidiousness in one brief comparison! It is not easy to be that precisely evocative. The tinkling of a harpsichord would have seemed too aristocratic for his context. The tinkling of a piano would have suggested a piano in a bar or a piano out of tune. The adjective "worn-out" keeps musical box from seeming too luxurious to apply to Mr. Charrington, who was poor or seemed so at that time in the novel. The author watched every possibility of his image.

Try a number of sentences that begin "to talk to him was like listening to" and see what you can suggest through various comparisons. Let a few be wacky or incomplete. Let some go out of control, and try to make one just right.

It may be fairly clear that a comparison lacking the words "like" or "as" is a metaphor:

- He is a prince among men.
- She is a pearl among peas.

The man is not literally a prince; the woman is not literally a pearl.

He has qualities of generosity and magnanimity associated with ideal princes. Her rare qualities make other people seem common beside her. That type of metaphor offers few difficulties.

Unconscious metaphors offer students more trouble than intended metaphors.

Geoffrey of Monmouth injected chivalry into the Round Table.

The reader sees a man crouching by a wooden table with a hypodermic labeled "chivalry." The verb "injected" was the trouble, too metaphoric to use on a table.

The ship of state split on the rock of his ambitions and dissolved them.

Here, the problem is the mixed metaphor. First the ship splits; it is made of wood. Then it dissolves his ambitions; it must be made of liquid, presumably sea water.

He bathed in the thumps and groans issuing from his stereo, letting the anguished wails pour over him, revelling in electronic miseries, as he swam upward toward some glorious height in a high dive of ecstatic flight.

Now he's flying, yet. He started by bathing, then showered, then began to swim upward, to dive, and then took off and flew. Granted poetic license, stick to one sport at a time.

Sometimes the trouble with metaphors is not just their inconsistency, but their excess as well.

His giant gaze included all Europe. All knowledge was his kingdom. With one arm he reached for the ancient power of Asia. With another he studied trade with Africa and the Near East. Like a colossus, he bestrode the continents, bending like a great protector to shield the weak and yet to encourage the adventurous by the insatiable curiosity that led him to stare at the heavens nightly through the new telescope.

His reaching, gazing, bestriding, bending, staring (while bent over?)

in two directions at once make him pretty athletic. (How did he study trade with one arm?)

> **He rocked the boat of her life in the tempests of his passion until the oceans of life overwhelmed her.**

Underline all the words using boat and water imagery. No wonder she drowned.

Those were all examples of metaphoric, or nonliteral, speech that went out of control because they were imperfectly imagined. Picture the words as you write them to prevent injecting a hypodermic into the Round Table.

Are There Any Rules About Metaphors and Similes?

None exist, but you might try a few suggestions. Try to keep your main subject dominant and the comparison subordinate, so that your central topic is not forgotten and the comparison serves to clarify it. To avoid the cliché concentrate on making the simile or metaphor as true or as accurate as possible. Keep an eye on the implication of the comparison—that is, what is suggested as well as what is said directly. You wouldn't usually call a baby's hand as soft as the skin of a worm. Why not? A worm's skin is soft, isn't it? What has that simile forgotten? Use metaphors and similes primarily to clarify your meaning, to make vivid and entertaining a difficult or elusive idea, not to call attention to your own writing.

How Should I Choose a Tone?

As a style is chosen for a purpose, a tone is chosen: encouraging, threatening, gentle, engaging, genial, angry, insistent, exasperated. Sometimes the tone will seem to appear on your pages without your conscious selection, but, often, establishing a tone may not be that easy. Whatever tone is needed for persuasion, try to achieve it. The encouraging tone that a dean might use to put heart in fearful freshmen would not be the appropriate tone in dealing with students who had broken into the bookstore and stolen from the cash registers.

You, as writer, must analyze what tone will be effective in order to choose the right one. Sincerity and spontaneity usually are not enough.

But What Tone Is Right for a Student's Paper?

There is no one right tone for any paper, student's or professional's, but probably the best tone for the individual student is the one that most nearly represents his actual relation to the material and to his audience. Three matters are involved: the individual student (his personality, interests, experience, skills, degree of self-confidence), his relation to his material (his subject or topic), and his relation to his audience (class, newspaper audience, unknown reader, a "new" teacher or one with whom he has studied before). All of these will determine his attitude as he writes. His attitude will be communicated more-or-less continuously as the paper's tone through his word choice. (Tone can, of course, be varied throughout a paper.)

Unless you are an expert on your topic, you cannot adopt the "we are all experts here together" manner and discourse with smooth elegance about the Victorians, as if your right foot rested on some fireside grate and your left hand held a wine glass. That is our romantic picture of scholars talking together, anyway. Nor should you write in the "I am a mere nothing" manner, with superhumble modesty, as if you had not a crumb to offer at the banquet of learning. False modesty is as inappropriate to all your recent labors as is false confidence.

If the Student Aims for a Quiet, Unassuming Tone, How Does He Select the Words to Suggest That?

If a student wishes his paper to have a quiet, unassuming tone, there are two ways to approach this: one is by a kind of laymen's autohypnosis, and the other is pure selectivity. Both are useful. For the first, before writing, sit and think a moment of your role as speaker of the paper. You are no longer a child in the company of "grown-ups." Nor are you a life-time expert conversing with learned colleagues. What, in fact, is your relation to this subject? Have you always been interested in it? Is it a new interest? Do you hate the topic, and need just to do this job and get it over, meanwhile trying to conceal your distaste from the audience? This last attitude and its problems would be important to have clear in your mind before starting. If you find the subject fascinating but aspects of it baffling or difficult, try to articulate this to yourself. It often is important to admit in the paper, when you reach the difficult section, that this problem is difficult or baffling. First, make your own relation to the subject as clear as possible to yourself.

Probably you do not feel like an expert and wish you did. Probably your paper has been the product of concentrated effort, and you still have doubts about sections of it. You know that <u>work</u> plus <u>time</u> does not equal <u>excellence,</u> but you know, as well, the evidence that your interpretations rest upon. In short, you are a person (not an ignoramus or an expert) writing as well as you can, without pretentions to eloquence, at the moment, on a subject you have long considered. If what you say is good, you are glad, but you do not claim it is the last word, and, granted some time, you may improve on it yourself. So much for autohypnosis.

Now, for pure selectivity. Earlier pages have treated pomposities of language, when, for example, "Mary had a little lamb" was expressed in bureaucratic jargon (p. 10). There are words a writer may choose that will suggest impressiveness and massive learning, and words that will imply a modest relation to self, subject, and audience, yet both can communicate the same information. The only way to vary tone and style as you wish in relation to your purpose is to increase your consciousness of the potentialities of individual words and what they suggest to you and to others. These problems of style and tone—called "usage," "diction," "linguistic acumen," or what you will—are problems, essentially, of word choice.

In order to avoid pompousness on one hand and excessive humility on the other, the plain style is probably the best goal. George Orwell, a great advocate of the plain style, gives six good guides:

- Never use a metaphor, simile or other figure of speech which you are used to seeing in print.
- Never use a long word where a short one will do.
- If it is possible to cut a word out, always cut it out.
- Never use the passive where you can use the active.
- Never use a foreign phrase, a scientific word or a jargon word if

you can think of an everyday English equivalent.

- Break any of these rules sooner than say anything outright barbarous.[19]

Orwell's rules lead inevitably to a plain, unpretentious style that still permits the writer to be emphatic and definite.

toward
a brisker pace

Are There Any Specific Hints that Help Increase the Pace of Prose?

Granted the great range of purposes for writing and subjects, Orwell's rules for the plain style, with some additions, help speed up the pace of prose as they pare away at the wordy style.

Choose simple words over multisyllabic, or supposedly impressive, words. Orwell's rule about never using a long word where a shorter one will do has important effects. It tends to make writing simpler, clearer, more concrete. This is not to say that all young writers do not need to keep adding to their vocabularies in order to have the perfect word at hand when they need it, but all writers must insist on the right word, not the bigger word—the word that precisely expresses the nuance one means, not the inflated and imprecise word that "sounds good."

A particularly mad use of Roget's *Thesaurus* is fairly well known among students. They write out their compositions and then translate them carefully word for word, using Roget's *Thesaurus,* into a lofty Martian English.

- "He was to be drafted" becomes "He was impressed into service."
- "She was gardening all weekend" becomes "She pursued her horticultural interests during the weekend."
- "He wanted to be a doctor, and when he got a bad mark in chemistry, he was worried and wrote his teacher to ask her to change his mark" becomes "Upon observation that his aspirations to enter the medical profession would be seriously threatened by his having received an unsatisfactory report in chemistry, he communicated with his teacher by mail and requested that she reconsider his term report."

In this last example, the first sentence was unglamorous, but the second was exhausting. Try for something between the two. If the heavy "tion" nouns are dropped and the adjectival material is put before the subject, the sentence will seem simpler and smoother:

> Wishing to become a doctor, but anxious about his low mark in chemistry, he wrote his teacher and asked her to reconsider the grade.

The sentence is not gorgeous now, because it is probably overpacked with information, but it is, at least, clearer.

In general, avoid the use of nouns that end in "tion" and "ment" wherever you can. They are useful, but when overused, they drag a passage down to a walk. The reader grapples to find the writer's meaning and often just quits.

> The abolition of the establishment of regulations concerning the development of new classes was avoided. (That one is almost impossible to understand, helped along by the passive form of the verb, too. Shift the subject and try it again.)
> The college senate avoided abolishing the rules about developing new classes. (Much better. If "developing" could be dropped, the sentence would be smoother, but to be fair, all the material of the earlier sentence had to stay.)

54

Vividness is always gained by any movement toward concreteness and away from abstraction. Nouns with "tion" and "ment" are, by nature, abstractions. Which is more vivid of these two sentences?

The increase of knowledge is proportionate to the degree of expenditure of effort.
You learn more if you work harder.

Those two sentences are stylistic extremes: the first, ponderous jargon, and the second, conversational. Suppose you wished more formality, some sentence between those two:

Understanding rises with effort expended.

The five nouns of the earliest sentences have been reduced to two, and the sentence feels taut without those "of" phrases sticking all the nouns together.

Take these two passages and rewrite them in the simplest words you can find. Drop whatever abstract nouns and "of" phrases you can:

- Yet in spite of the pressure of mechanization, in spite of the depletion and even the depression of the human personality, the creative arts have not altogether disappeared from our society.[20]
- Her reservation does not concern his capacity to do good but his ability to control the impulse toward self-gratification irrespective of consequences.[21]

For fun and practice the other way, try pushing these simple sentences up into the stratosphere:

- He ran away from home.
- His family was always trying to make him do things he did not want to do.
- She decided, no matter what her family said, to be a lawyer.
- Some people hate exercise.

Like Mary and her lamb, wherever the abstractions go, the passive verb is sure to follow. Regulations are usually established, operations undergone, investigations promulgated, traditions perpetuated, and so on. But common sense shows that the active verb is acting, vivid, lively, and the passive verb is limp, acted upon. The active verb jumps, runs, shouts, laughs, and the passive verb is beaten, jumped on, seen, struck, bothered, badgered, and finally buried. "They built a house" is the active form of the verb. "A house was built by them" is the passive form. "He seeks"; "It was sought." "She threw the ball"; "The ball was thrown by her." "They welcomed their guests"; "The guests were welcomed by them." "The dog bit him"; "He was bitten by the dog." In each of these paired sentences, the first sentence is active because the subject (they, he, she, they, dog, respectively) does the action (built, seeks, threw, welcomed, bit). In all of the second sentences, the verb is passive because the subject is acted upon; that is, it receives action but does not do it (was built, was sought, was thrown, were welcomed, was bitten).

Avoid Mary and her lamb, the abstractions and their attendant passive verbs, where you can, and the pace of your essay will increase as your writing becomes more lively and interesting. But, after all, abstractions and passive verbs are learned and literate vices, advanced errors that the uneducated rarely make. Some people will say, "Therefore, don't go to school," a silly comment, because abstractions sometimes are vital to us and often save words. For the one word "expedient," for example, you would have to say, "What you do in order to bring about a desired result." Synonyms for "expedient" are "device," "resource," "means," but "expedient" has moments of usefulness. Words, themselves, are abstractions, of course. We say "tree" and do not have to lug a "tree" into the room to convey to our neighbor what we mean. But some words allude to ideas for which there is no "tree," no object that one could cart in a sack for demonstration. "Freedom," "truth," "belief," "liberty," "illusion" are all such words. There is no thing in the world that is one of those. Rather, we abstract, draw out of many experiences, the idea of what illusions are. Or we may say, "That is an example of belief motivating a man's actions" or "There, the battle to retain freedom of intellectual life continued for years." All of these abstract words require definition and careful use, but we need them. Life without abstractions would be without spiritual, intellectual, or imaginative activity.

Avoid unnecessary words. You will be amazed at the brisk pace that you will gain merely by taking out "filler phrases," repetitive phrases, procedural transitions. "Filler phrases" are the extra words and phrases like "in consideration of," "in relation to," "the fact was that," "in the case of," "unusual in nature," "in respect to," "the reason was that." Begin to count words. Be pleased with yourself for writing ten words for fifteen and six for ten. It is possible to write an overpacked sentence that needs loosening up in order to give clarity. But the most usual student error is the overloose, imprecise sentence.

Probably because many students imitate speech, they will write, "A boy that hadn't been around school before asked how to find the auditorium." The one word "new" can work instead of six words there, "A new boy asked how to find the auditorium." The passage is speeded up.

> **The person who gets very angry one minute and sweet-talks the next is not much of a hit around here. (21 words)**
> **The erratic, emotional person is not trusted here. (8 words)**

If you don't like the compressed formality of that expression, loosen it up with something like this:

> **People around here don't like the person who shouts one moment and sweet-talks the next. (16)**

In that sentence you save words by finding a verb to stand for "who gets angry one minute" that will be parallel to "sweet-talks"; "shouts" will do.

For the clauses that make a sentence loose, try to find one word. For "the car that was painted red," "the red car." For "the street that had all kinds of garbage in it," "the littered street"; or try to describe it fully and say precisely what the litter was.

How would you tighten these loose sentences?

- The people who don't know what they are doing shouldn't run things.
- The stores that sell all kinds of things for the house are fun to walk around in sometimes.
- He wound up the toys, and then he let them go, and they went all over the place.
- He had one of those radios you can carry and had the wired

thing in his ear so that he could hear the ball game without bothering the people who had come to the library to study.

Tautology is the repetition of an idea in different words within a sentence, for example, "the necessary essentials," "basic fundamentals," "the exact same," "uniquely original," "high quality of excellence," "to consider mentally." The writer is repeating himself, usually without knowing it. Frequently we speak in tautologies or repetitive phrases because we are watching another person's face for reaction, and when there is none, we repeat, watching for a response: "He does not seem to be able to communicate . . . to say what he means," we say, repeating the word "communicate" by the last five words. In writing, aim to avoid tautologies. A listener cannot rehear, but a reader can reread.

Avoid procedural transitions like this: "But first, in order to make X clear, one should speak of Y for a moment." If X cannot be clear without Y, by all means explain Y, but there is no need to say that you must beforehand. The reader does not have to know all the writer's decisions, plans, and procedures. He presumes the writer has his reasons for his methods. If the methods do not work, then the reader has a right to grumble.

Sometimes, "Before we discuss . . . we should turn for a moment to . . ." is the writer's way of inserting a transition to the second topic: "Before we discuss Baldwin's essays we might speak of his early experience." That sentence manages the transition, but like a mechanical crane—by hoisting the reader in the air and setting him down before the new topic. Aim to make your transitions almost invisible. Is there nothing in Baldwin's early experience that influenced his essays? Of course, there is, or you would not be wishing to discuss it before you treat his essays. Find some key attitude or value, and use it as transition to link the two topics.

Undoubtedly his early experience provided adequate reasons for the defiant bitterness, even rage, of his later novels and essays. But his early experience also gave him the respect for his own intellect that he needed to survive and to express his fury brilliantly.

Now this writer can talk about the early experience and begin to link it with the later works. When you are caught without a way to reach your next topic and you need to write the mechanical-crane transition, something is wrong. The paragraphs need rearranging, or you have lost the focus of your main idea—Baldwin's development, for example.

Avoid the lecture style of "we see" or "we turn to" in an essay. "And thus we see" is a typical phrase from the stuffy, stilted essay that must be imitating the lecture hall, where the professor stands behind a lectern five hundred feet from his students, and the students yawn and wish they were outside. "In short," "briefly," "finally," "in conclusion," "to summarize"—any of these will do the job of "and thus we see." For "thus," try "therefore," and leave "thus" for sermons and the scriptural diction of the King James Version of the Bible, where it seems appropriate, richly formal and dressed in purple. The "we may now turn to" is a clumsy reaching for a transition, and both the "we" and the "turning" should go. As a general rule, use "we" only when you mean it; we Americans, we humans tend to do this and that. The editorial "we" is correct in formal papers, but it tends to be overused by inexperienced writers. Instead of "we," try other means, particularly the direct declarative sentence with a subject in the third person. Instead of "We know that the astronauts must train like athletes to endure privations of all sorts"; "The astronauts must train . . . ."

In summary, all the suggestions that serve to develop the plain style will also help to speed up the pace of your prose: choose active verbs over passive, simple words over multisyllabic; avoid excessive use of abstract nouns ending with "tion" and "ment"; delete extra words and phrases of all sorts, including tautologies; avoid unnecessary procedural transitions; and avoid the lecture style of "we see" and "we turn to."

Follow the five suggestions given for speeding up prose, and rewrite this passage as if you were a camp counselor giving a monthly report. The first sentence might be this simple: "Often the campers went on weekly trips."

It was often found to be customary for the campers to be led on various expeditions for weekly activities. Participational activities like canoe practicing on the lake with ongoing developmental activities like the practice of the various strokes, "the pull-to" and the "push-away," "the bow-sweep" and "the J-stroke" were found to be enthusiastically received by the interested campers. We see from this experience that participational activities are more favorably received than the nonparticipational ones like the observation of ping-pong or table-tennis matches or the viewing of races on the river, which seem to have drawn small audiences.

toward
a clearer focus

Are There Specific Ways to Keep Focus on the Subject?

TRANSITIONAL WORDS

Short transitional words, to be discussed again later (p. 100 ff), help to keep the reader following your thought closely. Sometimes you may include a transitional word in every sentence of a paragraph. Until you are comfortable with a variety of transitional words and phrases, you might develop a list to use for reference.

- To express agreement of one element with something expressed earlier: "in addition," "moreover," "also," "another"
- For an idea in contrast: "although," "but," "on the other hand," "however," "others say," "unlike"
- To return to your own position: "still," "actuality," "nonetheless," "nevertheless."

The very process or expanding these lists will increase your consciousness of words and their logical possibilities. What words might you use to grant a point to the opposition?

INTRODUCTIONS OF QUOTATIONS

Use that moment of introducing a quotation to help hold the paper's focus, to remind your reader of the reasons he is to read that quotation. Say something helpful about the quotation before you present it, so the reader will look for that idea in the quotation. Otherwise, if you explain the purpose of the quotation after you present it, the reader must go back and reread the passage to see if he grasps your idea. If an introduction says only "The author presents the scene," the reader has no hint of any characteristic to be observed in the scene. The reader is prepared to observe what two subjects by this introduction: "Clark uses colorful, active verbs to describe his mission."

If the primary focus is held steady by the introduction to the quoted passage, then the quotation can be used to demonstrate additional points. After it is quoted, the writer may repeat briefly the reason for the quotation, but then he can move on to remark on something else illustrated in the same passage. A passage from an imaginary paper illustrates this double use:

> Clark uses colorful, active verbs describing his mission: "We swung around the bend in the river and suddenly faced the rapids. The canoe bucked and slid as it shot toward the white foaming water. Gerald grabbed my arm and whispered that Ralph wasn't up to this." All those verbs—swung, faced, bucked, slid, shot, grabbed, even whispered—are active, energetic words that help portray the adventure and the energy of the narrator, Clark. Although Clark does not stress his own importance, it is clear that Gerald depends on him. Gerald is full of fears himself, and his fear that Ralph is not "up to this" could be expressed just as accurately of him. In fact, all of Clark's energy and diplomacy were needed to navigate the Green River and to deal with Gerald's fear and Ralph's fits of depression.

The quoted material shows the active, colorful verbs first and suggests Clark's energy. The content, then, shows Clark being depended on and permits the writer to move toward his next subject, how Clark coped with the mission.

Be sure to keep the quoted material and your introduction as one grammatical unit.

> **The counterfeiter had high standards; he said that "I always use only the very best engraving and the highest quality of paper."**

The introducing sentence is in indirect discourse (he said that he would), but the material quoted is a direct quotation (called also direct discourse). To be correct the passage would have to run one of two ways:

- The counterfeiter had high standards. He said that he always used only the best engraving and the highest quality of paper.
- The counterfeiter had high standards. He said, "I always use only the very best engraving and the highest quality of paper."

In the next example, the writer holds to Mark Twain's pattern and introduces his material, making it clear who speaks:

> **Huckleberry Finn tells of Jim's shrewd advice: "Jim said if we had the canoe hid in a good place, and had all the traps in the cavern, we could rush there if anybody was to come to the island, and they would never find us without dogs."** [22]
> **Huckleberry listened to Jim's advice: "Jim said if we had the canoe hid . . . ."**

That form would do as well because the quote illustrates Huck's attention. But the following passage is less clear.

> **Jim often advised Huckleberry: "Jim said if we had the canoe hid . . . ."**

The introduction ("Jim often advised Huckleberry") suggests that Jim will speak in the quoted material, but instead Huckleberry speaks, telling what Jim had said. Momentarily the reader is confused.

revising

Why Revise? Isn't Spontaneity Best?

About some things, spontaneity may be best as it is better to go swimming when you are hot or to eat when you are hungry, but what is written as a "spontaneous overflow of powerful feelings" probably will need revising in order to make what is genuine, truly seem so. The intensely genuine has a way of seeming sloppy and self-indulgent when it remains untrimmed. Shelley's "Oh lift me from the grass! I die! I faint! I fail!" may have been sincere and passionately experienced by him, but it leaves us embarrassed. We wish he would get up off the grass. It is too directly expressed to communicate its emotion. Further, although spontaneity is usually considered a measure of feeling and healthy naturalism, it is no indicator of accuracy or even of depth of feeling as it is usually assumed to be. It is true that what is written out of an urgent wish to articulate and recreate experience may please the writer enormously at the time of writing; still, it will need to be reconsidered later and probably be given a more general application.

There are other reasons to revise. In the writing process, the balance goes off sometimes, and the author may overdevelop one section and undertreat another. He may use too many examples of one sort—perhaps too many from interviews and too few from secondary sources. He may have forgotten to include items. All writing needs the later, more objective review and revision for balance and perspective, in order to sharpen a focus, clarify a phrase, tighten relationships between sentences and paragraphs, and work toward a brisk pace and firm emphasis.

Should Every Writer Expect to Have to Revise?

Yes, every piece of writing is revisable. A writer should look forward to at least one revision and prepare for it by making little marks on his first draft indicating where he hopes to revise. To prepare to revise, it is helpful to type or write the first draft skipping three spaces between lines. After the first writing, the paper's strengths and flaws show up clearly, and you can be quite enthusiastic about the first rewriting and the first corrections, partly because they will seem so obvious to you.

How Do I Prepare for the Second Draft?

Everyone develops his or her own method. Some people prefer to read for continuity first and some prefer to do this second, but here is one procedure. If you can, give the paper a day or two—or even a week or more—to enable you to gain some distance and perspective on it. Then give it a swift rereading. Pretend that you are reading a stranger's paper, and with this attempt at genuine objectivity, read rapidly for logical continuity. Is your thesis clear? Do the paragraphs seem to follow one another in a logical order? Reread topic sentences of paragraphs alone rapidly to double check for the logical sequence of paragraphs. As you read, use a contrasting pencil to note oddities of expression for later correction. Put question marks for matters that seem unclear, crosses for incorrect expression.

When paragraphs seem to be out of order, you might draw arrows or use numbers to indicate their new place, or you might draw a *V* on its side for inserts. Expect to make changes, and use whatever signs are helpful.

After the first quick reading to check on continuity and the general logical movement of the paper, give the paper a very slow reading. Try to be like a sieve in a sandpile, catching every alien particle: every error of punctuation or grammar, every extra word and phrase. Watch for extra adjectives, repetitive phrasing. Now those extra spaces above the lines will be useful for insertions. Do you see any clichés? Put in a fresher, more vivid and more accurate phrase. Write corrections above the lines if possible, or, using insert signals, rewrite rough places on another sheet of paper. Don't write new material on the back of the composition paper. Additions often turn out to be longer than expected. If your addition exceeds the length of the back of the page you will have to write it elsewhere and unnecessary confusion can follow. Now the paper is probably such a mess that you will be glad to retype it so that you can see it more clearly.

Depending on how you count, you are now at the first or second reworking. You are looking at a retyped and reworked first draft, a revised paper. Give it the usual fast and slow rereading. Then, if it is logical, if its paragraphs move in sequence, if it is grammatical, it is time to concentrate seriously on the paper's pace. To do this, use every method you know. If you can, spark the verbs by adding color, and drop ''there is,'' ''it is,'' and passives. Tighten those connections between sentences and paragraphs by adding transitional words that express the logical relationships, if you need them. Take out any ungainly or slow introducers and write helpful, informative introducers that tip off the reader to your central reason for quoting the passage. Drop any word or phrase that does not seem to pull its weight in the sentence. Are there any fillers left? Can you cut out any piece of information, any extra adjective? When your text is amusing, is it brief enough?

Then, give the quoted passages and footnotes another check. Are all quoted passages absolutely true to the original, down to the author's every punctuation mark? Check your quotations once more against the originals, and be sure to check the page numbers at the same time. Professional writers place such importance on this kind of accuracy that they often hire someone to go to the library with their finished article in hand to make their final check.

Take one last look at the conclusion. Is it clear, emphatic enough? Does it pick up every major point of the paper and carry out what the introduction hinted? If you are satisfied, it may be time to stop. Perhaps you have two more papers to do before the end of the term. Now it is probably time to type the paper up for its last time and hand it in.

When Should I Stop Revising?

A paper at the fifteenth revision could still, theoretically, be revised. But you cannot go on seeing new things wrong with your own paper without time lapses to gain perspective between reviews. Anyone gets tired of the old thing. Another perspective is needed, some friend to be a constructive critic, or more time to regain your own objectivity. Practically speaking, there is a point of diminishing returns when priorities have to be considered. Will you get enough out of the time spent on this revision to be worth it, when the same time might be spent preparing for some new project? Considering all the growing to be done in these years, after the second draft has been thoroughly revised, a student's study time would be better spent moving on to new reading and new research than in reworking a third draft. Some students get themselves stuck in the rut of continuously revising, but most refuse to revise at all. The first group can avoid judgment by never letting the work be finished, and the second can avoid self-scrutiny by saying that they never really tried. Try to avoid both these evasions by doing what time, energy, and your own demands of yourself require, then, in peace, put the work aside and go on to something new. For the professional, the work may have to undergo many more revisions, depending on his own standards, those of his editors, and the space permitted him. For most students' purposes a corrected first draft, typed or written up to hand in (called a third draft) is realistic and sufficient to provide the growth that the teacher planned for that one piece of work.

NOTES FOR PART 1

1. Alexander Pope, "Essay on Criticism," *Selected Poetry and Prose,* ed. William K. Wimsatt, Jr. (New York: Holt, Rinehart and Winston, 1963), ll. 215–218.

2. John Fischer, "The Easy Chair: Open Letter to the Next President," *Harper's,* Sept. 1968, pp. 12 and 20.

3. John Kenneth Galbraith, "The Day Krushchev Visited the Establishment," *Harper's,* Feb. 1971, p. 75.

4. Henry James, "Project of the Novel by Henry James," in *The Ambassadors,* ed. S. P. Rosenbaum (New York: W. W. Norton, 1964), pp. 376–77.

5. John Henry Cardinal Newman, "The Idea of a University," in *Relevants,* ed. Edward Quinn and Paul J. Dolan (New York: The Free Press, 1970), p. 379.

6. Piri Thomas, *Down These Mean Streets* (New York: New American Library, 1967), p. 119.

7. Dick Francis, *Enquiry* (New York: Berkley Medallion Books, 1969), p. 7.

8. Flannery O'Connor, "Wise Blood," in *Three by Flannery O'Connor* (New York: New American Library, 1962), p. 11.

9. William Shakespeare, *Henry the Fifth,* ed. William Allan Neilson and Charles Jarvis Hill (Cambridge: The Riverside Press, 1942), IV, iii, 41–67.

10. John Oliver Killens, "Explanation of the 'Black Psyche'," in *From a Black Perspective,* ed. Douglas A. Hughes (New York: Holt, Rinehart and Winston, 1970), pp. 71–2.

11. Gael Greene, "Into the Mouths of Babes," *New York Magazine,* 21 June 1971, p. 73.

12. Green, "Babes," p. 73.

13. "The Freeze That Pleases," *Time,* 21 June 1971, p. 76.

14. Joseph Conrad, *Heart of Darkness,* ed. Robert Kimbrough (New York: W. W. Norton, 1963), p. 59.

15. Conrad, *Darkness,* p. 72.

16. George Orwell, *1984* (New York: New American Library, 1961), p. 16.

17. Orwell, *1984,* p. 101.

18. Orwell, *1984,* p. 125.

19. George Orwell, "Politics and the English Language," in *Modern Essays on Writing and Style,* ed. Paul C. Wermuth (New York: Holt, Rinehart and Winston, 1964), p. 108.

20. Lewis Mumford, "The Role of the Creative Arts in Contemporary Society," in *Writer and Audience: Forms of Non-Fiction Prose,* ed. Wilson Currin Snipes (New York: Holt, Rinehart and Winston, 1970), p. 159.

21. Jean Frantz Blackall, "Perspectives on Harold Frederic's *Market Place,"* *PMLA,* 86 (1971), 397.

22. Mark Twain, *The Adventures of Huckleberry Finn* (New York: Harper & Brothers, 1912), p. 75.

organization and paragraph development

introductions

How Do I Start the Paper?

Introductions are probably the most difficult part of the paper to write. Some people write three pages before they finally say their introduction, and then they go back and cut out those first three pages. To clarify it, put the question differently: "What does the introduction do?" It introduces your paper, not all of modern literature, all of existentialist thought, all of Camus' works, *The Stranger* as a novel—but your paper and its ideas on *The Stranger*. The introductory paragraphs might suggest why the subject is important and what have been other approaches to the subject, but the last line of the first or second paragraph should express quite firmly the author's thesis. Some teachers require the rather heavy-footed, "This paper will aim to demonstrate that . . . ." If an editor or teacher considers that good practice, one must bow, but the firm declarative sentence of interpretation placed strategically should announce the author's intentions to the attentive reader.

Without saying, "This paper will treat X and Y before going on to Z," the introduction should suggest broadly the paper's plan. "Among all the reforms needed at our school, the first should be an increase in student interest and participation at all levels." A paper with that line in its introduction is obviously going to treat the reforms needed at school, student apathy, and it is probably going to suggest that students would not be so apathetic if they were more involved in making decisions. Although the paper may contain many surprises, nothing in it should be alien to its introduction. The author does not have to treat everything an introduction implies, but nothing it does treat should be outside the scope of the introductory paragraph. In short, the introduction needs to be broad enough in its expression of themes and topics so that the entire paper may be drawn from it.

The introduction may have to be revised often to be focused more sharply, or to include a general idea that the paper develops. Some people advocate writing the introduction last, but the task of writing it first is useful, because often it reveals to the author his indefiniteness of focus, and it is better to realize vagueness early than late. One teacher of writing, Sheridan Baker, suggests that the author consider the introductory paragraphs as an inverted funnel from broad generalization to narrow thesis statement. That concept is useful, provided the generalizations are not so broadly stated that the student offers himself as an authority on matters that are beyond him. If he has studied ten of Shakespeare's sonnets carefully, he cannot pretend to be an authority on the Renaissance or on all of Shakespeare's works. He is prepared to say something about the general interest and significance of the sonnets as he works toward his thesis statement: "A selection of the sonnets reveals Shakespeare's intense concern about X."

For a moment, think of the introduction in terms of a movie. In a sense, the introduction is like a camera's broad-angled picture of the countryside as it narrows and moves in toward a village and then to a house and to a room in the house where two people are talking during breakfast. Many introductions include too much of the countryside. Perhaps they should begin with the filmshot of the village. If the writer begins too far back from his subject, he is, in effect, introducing his introduction, like this:

> Unquestionably the Renaissance was one of the most creative
> periods in history, and the greatest dramatist of the Renaissance

74

was Shakespeare. In his own time, his plays were "hits," and in ours, they are presented all over the world to select audiences and to hoards of groundlings in public parks. Students have loved him and laughed over his clowns; professors have smiled at his witticisms; lovers have sighed over his touching insights. But his sonnets, rarely considered by the masses, but much admired by the cognoscenti, are not used as fully as they might be to indicate his interests and concerns before the time he wrote his plays. It is believed that he wrote most of his 154 sonnets before 1597. An examination of *Love's Labours Lost* shows Shakespeare's great interest in the sonnet form, and comparison of that play with selected early sonnets suggests certain similarities of themes.

The first two sentences should be omitted because they are obvious and irrelevant to the thesis as it is finally stated in the last sentence. The third sentence should be cut mainly because it is cliché-ridden and condescending. No one laughs much at the clowns as he reads Shakespeare, although the clowns may be funny on stage. Professors can be spared consideration as dried up old crochets, and no one thinks of lovers sighing in that romantic haze anymore. The introduction should begin at "His sonnets, rarely considered by the masses," and, with the elimination of the intellectual snobbery "masses" versus "cognoscenti," should proceed beyond "indicates certain similar themes." The introduction to the school or college paper should state what the "certain similarities of themes" are quite specifically. The introduction of the journalistic essay might begin as far back as the first sentence, and probably it would not proceed to the enumeration of the "similar themes." Perhaps the central reason for this difference is the factor of audience interest.

Shouldn't I Try to Interest the Reader Through my Introduction?

Indeed, interesting the reader is an important factor in all introductions, but the writer should not underestimate the reader's ability to be interested by intelligent ideas. A packed introduction that presents ideas in rapid succession—the paper's subject, its significance, the author's method of approach, and his central thesis—will engage the reader's interest.

Writers for magazines, however, cannot count on being read

as students can. Their audiences are uncomfortable commuters on a train whose air conditioning is not working, or mothers trying to read under the dryer as their nails are being manicured, or patients nervously flipping pages in a dentist's office. Introductions for that preoccupied audience may have to suggest something more directly engaging, like this:

> "COME AND GET REACQUAINTED," the mimeographed sheet said. "Concord Rod and Gun Club. Strawberry Hill Road . . . Smorgasbord Dinner, Dancing, and Chatting . . . SEE YOU THERE!"
>
> The invitation summoned me to the twenty-fifth reunion of the Concord High School Class of 1945, and I decided, somewhat to my surprise, I wanted to go. I had always remembered, with embarrassing clarity, a rather difficult adolescence in Concord, and now, trying to rediscover my own past, I hoped to find out what the surviving evidence of youth could reveal to the observation of middle age.[1]

Although the journalist may begin in a much more leisurely fashion, his structure, despite the appearance of casualness, is often as firm and tight as that of the apparently more orthodox academic paper:

> The Pentagon has just sent me Volume No. 70 of its official history of World War II— a painfully detailed account, in 491 pages, of the Italian campaign from the Salerno invasion to the fall of Cassino. Like the earlier volumes, it is a solid piece of work, researched from all known sources including the enemy's. So far as I can tell, it is accurate. It even records moments when American troops were less than heroic, and when famous generals made mistakes.
>
> Yet, as I read it, I kept feeling that something was missing. Finally it came to me: official histories make everything that happened sound rational, the end product of a logical chain of cause and effect. But to the people there at the time, these happenings seldom looked that way. More often they seemed downright zany, like scenes stolen from the theater of the absurd.[2]

Despite the relaxed manner, the author moved from a broad overview of the subject in his mention of Volume No. 70, his explanation of what that is and a general evaluation of it, to a narrow focus upon the aspect of the work that he would explore and present in his article.

But the introduction to a research paper for an academic audience can begin closer to its subject. John Hollow's essay published in *PMLA* (May 1971) asserts his central theme in the third sentence of the first paragraph:

> After he decided against a career in the Church (1855), William Morris was reluctant to talk about religion, called himself "careless of metaphysics and religion," and felt "no disposition to discuss them, because I find that such discussions inevitably become mere word-contests." Critics have assumed from this reluctance that Morris "wandered into the by-paths of agnosticism without any of the spiritual torments which usually accompanied loss of religious conviction among the Victorians." But a number of Morris' early stories and poems suggest that he was careless of metaphysics and religion because he thought men should not concern themselves about God.[3]

Notice how much ground that first paragraph covers. The first sentence sets the timing and the problems. The second says what "critics have assumed" from the conditions given in the first sentence. The third sentence, beginning "But a number . . . suggest," implies the author's disagreement with the critics and the grounds for his disagreement (evidence of early stories and poems), and it suggests his method of approach (to discuss the early stories and poems). Hollow does not say, "I plan to demonstrate that . . . ." Still, it is quite clear that Hollow will use the evidence of Morris' early stories and poems to show that he did not aimlessly wander "into by-paths of agnosticism" later in his life, but that his later agnosticism was based upon earlier convictions.

Still, the introductions witten for the academic and for the popular audience are quite similar in basic pattern. Both move from broad generalizations to the narrow focusing statement that will guide the paper toward its conclusion. Both present the general subject and the author's thesis statement, usually within the early paragraphs, but the journalistic essay can move in leisurely fashion toward the thesis statement and spend the time diverting its audience and engaging its interest. The academic paper is read for business, not primarily for pleasure, to inform the busy professional, for example, about William Morris, or some new theory about our economy, or a new design for contact lenses, or new procedures for job training for the unemployed.

The journalistic essay can employ so many varieties of approach that it is difficult to generalize, but somewhere in the early paragraphs, the journalistic essay will express its paper's subject and fulfill the requirements that the academic paper must fulfill more quickly. The journalist is under no obligation to state how he will demonstrate his theory or what other writers have thought, although he will suggest, probably at the outset why his subject is important. As you read in newspapers and magazines, watch the opening paragraphs, and try to be conscious of what they do, how they prepare the reader. Do they suggest untold wonders to follow? Do they depend on intellectual interest alone? Do they express the author's thesis generally or precisely? Are you sure at the end of the second paragraph what the paper's subject is? Do you feel that the writer has treated you as an intelligent person, or as a numbskull? Why does that matter?

the
middle
paragraphs

The total paper, research or nonresearch, journalistic or academic, is composed of paragraphs that move from the introduction to the conclusion. But paragraphs come in various sizes. Those in newspapers are narrow, short, often one sentence long, but paragraphs in books and magazines may be much longer. Is there any principle governing paragraph length?

What Is a Paragraph?

A paragraph is a series of sentences that expresses or describes one central idea. Since ideas may be divided into smaller and smaller units, or the idea of one paragraph may be expanded into an article or even a book, the notion of "one idea" has to be understood as relative to other ideas in the same composition. For example, in an essay describing a family's trials with the automobile, one paragraph could describe a series of incidents that occurred when three members of the family were learning to drive at the same time. Or in that same essay, the author might choose to write three paragraphs, one for each of the episodes concerning each driver's apprenticeship.

There is, in this way, no one idea that is obviously or inherently a one-paragraph idea. A writer decides what kind of development he wishes to give an idea within his total scheme. As he lists his ideas on a sheet of paper in outline, often their relative importance becomes clear. Again, one paragraph could describe father's brush with the police when he had forgotten to renew his license, or that same incident could be viewed as merely one bit of evidence in a paragraph showing how wise it was for father to withdraw himself from what he considered to be competition with other drivers. The paragraph is a useful convention that makes the author's thinking more accessible to the reader. By spacing on the page (indenting a paragraph) and by arranging a series of sentences together, you, as the author, announce to your reader what you consider to be one thought unit or one central idea.

How Does the Paragraph Relate to the Paper as a Whole?

A paragraph is one idea in a sequence of ideas, from thesis to summary. To get the feel of what a paragraph is, take a topic like sports and think of five reasons why you like or hate sports. Your introduction will announce the subject, tell your basic view of it, and broadly review your five reasons. Each of the five central paragraphs will expand upon one of these five reasons. The conclusion will summarize and repeat, with slight changes, the five reasons. That pattern, rigid as it is, is useful to have in mind in the early years of practice in writing expository essays.

Is There a Basic Pattern for the Expository Essay?

The body or central portion of the essay always expands upon the general ideas of the introduction. The conclusion usually recapitulates the essay's main points. The conclusion of one essay may consist of the five main reasons for wanting to travel; in another, the conclusion may be a restatement of one abstract idea, for example, Hollow's ideas on William Morris. Instead of five paragraphs on five reasons, many paragraphs of illustration and discussion may clarify the introductory paragraph. But the basic pattern—announcement of the subject and the author's view of the subject (introduction), followed by support through illustration, definition, explanation (body of paper), and finally the conclusion—will remain a useful pattern for all subjects treated in an expository essay.

Are All Paragraphs Developed in the Same Way?

Although there are many ways to develop paragraphs, all paragraphs aim to support their central ideas, usually expressed through a topic sentence. The topic sentence—like the essay's thesis statement which is built into the introductory paragraph—guides the main idea in the individual paragraph. It may guide the paragraph obviously by being placed first so that it is clear that every sentence in the paragraph offers support for it. Or the topic sentence can be placed last or even in the middle of the paragraph. Then, less obviously, but just as practically, the paragraph is organized around the topic idea. Whether that topic sentence is placed first or last or even left unexpressed, the paragraph moves toward demonstration or explanation of its central idea and toward the next paragraph, which will serve to support the thesis statement given in the introductory paragraph. An Xray of an essay might look like this:

Introduction	subject of paper
	its importance
	author's thesis
	author's method of approach
Central paragraphs	topic sentence
	several illustrations
	conclusion and transition

or	topic sentence
	discussion
	conclusion and transition
	contrasting idea developed
Body of Paper	topic sentence
	return to idea of paragraph 3
	topic sentence
	definition
	conclusion and transition
Conclusion	summary of main ideas of central paragraphs
	(Perhaps) analogy for restatement

What Are Some Types of Paragraph Development?

Perhaps the most useful method of paragraph development is the one that amplifies or expands upon the topic sentence. At first, it is wise to begin every paragraph with a topic sentence, and, indeed, the strong guiding topic sentence placed first in the paragraph always gives the paragraph the grace of clarity. In the method of development by amplification, the writer can support his topic sentence directly in one of four ways: by one illustration that he develops at length, by several illustrations that serve the same subject, by restatement in various ways, or by dividing up the topic idea, called analysis or classification.

DEVELOPMENT BY AMPLIFICATION: ONE EXAMPLE AND MANY

"Sportsmen are often bad sports" might be illustrated by one horrendous example showing a fine tennis player who was also a liar and a cheat on the court and an embezzler in private life. Or it might be illustrated by many examples of superb athletes whose values violated the view that sports build character. The notion of "traveling well prepared" is expanded on in this illustration, that of the French couple that takes a different item on each trip:

Alice told of her friends, the French couple, that believes in traveling well prepared. On each trip they take a new item just to see if the opportunity to use it might turn up. Last time a small piece of plastic and a coil of Scotch tape came in handy for mending the window in an old farmhouse where they happened to be marooned during an ice storm. They no longer carry the piece of flower pot and the metronome, having found no use for them in three trips. Although Alice says that she does not subscribe completely to their doctrine, I did notice that she had a small piece of twine with her to serve as a clothes line in her hotel room, or so she said.

In another paragraph developed by illustrations, the aunt's resourcefulness is demonstrated by many examples:

His aunt believes in being well prepared on picnics. Last time, she brought—along with the hot dogs—rolls, potato chips, Coke, and watermelon, mosquito netting to drape over the trees, a rubber inner tube, in case they found water to swim in, a trowel in case she found some sweet woodruff to bring home, a small cage with a falling portcullis to catch a rabbit for his younger brothers, lettuce for the rabbit to eat coming home in the car, and Pepto Bismol, not for the rabbit. As it happened, it rained, which she couldn't help. She pulled out a plastic tarpaulin (used to protect the trunk of the car from all the stuff she usually carries), and they had their picnic anyway in their tent by the side of the road.

The aunt's resourcefulness is shown here, really, by three basic illustrations: her preparedness for eating on the picnic, for activities after the picnic, and by her resourcefulness when it rained.

A freshman's paragraph on pollution was developed by examples:

Pollution is a dangerous threat to our world today. It affects every one of us every day of our lives. Industries and cars pour poisonous gases into the very air we have to breathe. This polluted air is a great health hazard, and if it goes unchecked the air will be totally unbreathable. The land that people thought would always be there is being damaged beyond repair, and our beaches are so polluted they are unsafe for people to bathe in. What kind of a legacy is this to leave for future generations? The industrial wastes and sewage dumped into our waters kill multitudes of marine life. A great number of animals in this country alone are on the verge of extinction because of man's carelessness and selfishness. Among these is our own national bird, the bald eagle. If pollution is allowed to continue unchecked as it is, man will destroy his own world. It is for these reasons that Americans must adopt a more sensible attitude towards pollution. One cannot afford to sit back and say let someone else worry about it.

—Karen Abbott

In the following example that appeared as the second paragraph in a speech, the topic idea—that prevailing curricula are developed for men students—is not expressed directly in the paragraph. The repeated illustrations, of the circumstance, however, express it fully:

Let us imagine a woman student entering college to major in English literature. In her freshman year she would probably study literature and composition, and the texts in her course would be selected for their timeliness, or their relevance, or their power to involve the reader, rather than for their absolute standing in the literary canon. Thus she might be assigned any one of the texts which have recently been advertised for Freshman English: an anthology of essays, perhaps such as the The Responsible Man, "for the student who wants literature relevant to the world in which he lives," or Conditions of Men, or Man in Crisis: Perspectives on the Individual and His World, or again, Representative Men: Cult Heroes of Our Time, in which the thirty-three men represent such categories of heroism as the writer, the poet, the dramatist, the artist, and the guru, and the only two women included are the Actress Elizabeth Taylor, and The Existential Heroine Jacqueline Onassis.[4]

That sequence of illustrations shows the male-oriented curriculum nicely—so well, in fact, that the writer could let the truth come home to the listener without asserting it directly in the paragraph. What topic sentence might be written for the paragraph?

DEVELOPMENT BY AMPLIFICATION: RESTATEMENT

Restatement also amplifies the topic sentence and usually by using illustrations as well:

New York City has been called cold, austere, impersonal, but in actuality it is the most individualistic of cities. What visitors take to be austerity or coldness is overwhelming vitality and, true, self-concern. Everyone is about his own business and does not wish to be diverted. If no one nods to you in the apartment elevator, do not be concerned. You are not invisible. If taxi drivers ignore your wave, they are swooping down on someone they saw first. Everyone has his own way to go and will dress as he pleases going there. If he chooses to walk on his hands along Park Avenue, no one will notice, unless he does it badly. Then a competiton may ensue. Bike riders now own the parks and will soon own the street. Secretaries and clerks sun themselves on the hot asphalt of city roofs. Teachers zoom into the universities and park their motorcycles outside, although their bicycles can travel the elevators up to faculty offices. Everyone is doing his own thing, as the kids say, and with his head full of plans, how can he see anyone else on the way? It is individualism not austerity or impersonality that pervades New York.

Here, individualism is restated by "about his own business," "everyone is doing his own thing," "it is individualism," and by the various examples, which illustrate "self-concern." You may see "individualism" as a more serious term than this, but an author is permitted to define or limit a term in his own context.

DEVELOPMENT BY AMPLIFICATION: CLASSIFICATION OR ANALYSIS

"Some people should never become drivers" is the kind of topic sentence that lends itself well to development by classification or analysis. By that method, the topic idea is divided into parts. In the following paragraph, bad drivers are divided into what groups?

Some people should never become drivers. Angry, hostile, and highly competitive people should be turned to other pursuits, calming ones like bathing and sailing or fishing. Those people who get jumpy when the great trucks come barreling down might be led to use service roads. Everyone becomes nervous at times, but the hysterical personality who begins flipping the indicator lights in the wrong directions under pressure should be diverted to public transportation. Most people are well enough coordinated to drive, and most people see well enough to drive, but, as the professor says in *My Fair Lady,* why can't they clean up the mess that's inside? Psychological tests that would select the angry, the hostile, the aggressive, the highly competitive, and the hysterical personalities would, people say, be opposed by Detroit, but, for that matter, tests might keep those wild car salesmen off the road as well.

Those impossible writing topics like "Two Kinds of People" and "Four Kinds of Readers" encourage generalizations that can be clever or funny but are rarely sound. Still, the technique is properly used if the connection between the generalization and the application appears close. For example, these topics clearly have an inherent affinity for development by classification: "Some trees are best for the wood used in indoor paneling"; "There are two kinds of 'first serves' in tennis: the hard flat serve and the high, spinning, bouncing serve"; "Some kinds of horses are built to carry weight"; "There are two good ways to fell a tree." Personally, I would avoid the "There are two (three, four, five, etc.) types of teachers (students, friends, husbands, houses, families, etc.)" statements. They are invitations for unavoidable oversimplifications; in other words, they lead writers to lie.

Two freshmen, Pedro Cortes and Brian McCormack, found good subjects to develop by classification.

DIFFERENT KINDS OF HIGHS

Mentally elevating oneself from worldly problems such as employment, family, and people is very common today and in some countries it is accepted. The use of different kinds of drugs for this purpose is, perhaps, the most popular among young people today. They can be seen walking around in a daze or just sleeping it off on some park bench. Likewise, these same people are read about on the front pages of newspapers, all paying the price for their brief time of relaxation. Similarly, others are involved in one form of meditation or another, all trying to escape or to find rest from our fast-moving society. With this objective in mind, people from all walks of life are engaging in different ways of getting high. While none of these offers any constructive outlet for their anxieties, they seem to be increasing day by day. However, one way of attaining a high and making contributions to our society is available to us all. Purely on opinion, I would say that the giving of oneself totally to some cause or struggle would be the best high of them all.

—Pedro Cortes

TWO KINDS OF FANS

There are mainly two kinds of sport fans, the loyal fan and the fickle fan. There is a very thin line between the two, but nonetheless, that line does exist. The fickle fan does not necessarily attend sporting events in person, but usually follows his team closely on the radio and TV. The fickle fan, when his team is winning, is a great cheerer and enthusiast of the team and when attending a game contributes much to the spirit of the team and the fans around him. When his team is victorious, he is ebullient and is the first one to congratulate his heroes. However, it is when his team is losing that the fickle fan shows his true colors. This type of fan can often be heard shouting such things as, "What are ya', blind? You call yourselves professionals? Where did ya' evah learn how ta play? Ya' bum!" and many other quaint little expressions. When attending a game, and his team is losing, he can be seen leaving the game before it is over. Now, the loyal fan doesn't necessarily attend live games either. As a matter of fact, the loyal fan is identical with the fickle fan except when it comes to his team's losing. Here is where the thin line of distinction shows between the two types. When a loyal fan's team is losing, he gets upset as much as the fickle fan, but the loyal fan realizes that his heroes are men and, as such, are bound to have bad nights. Realizing this, when his team starts losing, he cheers them on harder. And when it comes time for his team to meet defeat, he doesn't run away; he stays and watches and faces defeat with them. The loyal fan is a real fan, and in this age of synthetics, we need the real things of life.

—Brian McCormack

In using techniques of amplification, the writer holds to the topic sentence throughout and expands upon it by illustration, restatement, or classification. You can see that part of the development by classification might include discussion and comparison of the elements classified, as Mr. McCormack did with his fickle and loyal fans. By another, but related, method of paragraph development, called "development by comparison," the writer clarifies the topic sentence by comparison or contrast and draws a second concept or subject into the discussion. Sometimes the second subject is as important as the first, and sometimes it is subordinate.

DEVELOPMENT BY COMPARISON: WITH TWO EQUAL ELEMENTS

To lovers of the city life, the country seems slow and inefficient. One has to go to five stores to buy five items and to be sure to do so at the proper times between 9 and 5. In the city one can satisfy a yen for pizza at midnight, but in the country there may be no pizza anywhere for thirty miles or so. But lovers of the country do not mind missing the pizza. They say you can leave a car unlocked and find it there in the morning, or you can walk to the five stores without being mugged. They admit to the lack of concerts, plays, and ballet, but when a road company comes through everyone turns out and enjoys a fine evening. To this the city people would reply, "But we can go to a better performance almost any night we wish." The city/country argument is utterly insoluble. Like the argument about the mountains and the shore, it depends on whether you prefer the air or the swimming.

In that comparison the two elements were held equal. The author did not ridicule one and admire the other but admitted finally that preference depended upon priorities. Country people accept limitations of food, hours, and plays in return for safety and good air. To hold the two elements equal in importance, write one sentence for each side of the comparison, or use balancing words like "but," "however," "still," "the other view" to keep the two sides of the comparison steady in the reader's mind.

DEVELOPMENT BY CONTRAST: TWO ITEMS UNEQUAL

The relentlessly partisan paragraph loads the adjectives and oversimplifies the evidence:

There is no question that city living is intolerable. Any sane man would have his bag packed if he had a job to go to in the country. Who would choose city congestion over a small town with 264 post boxes working in the winter? Who would choose the bad air and the dangers of city living if he could have the sweet fragrance and the peace of country living? Of what value are all the so-called cultural benefits of the city if one is afraid to go home after them? It would be better to stay home in the country and turn out when your neighbors do to see the traveling ballet company when it comes to town. Unquestionably, the cities will have to become more fitted to human living, or they will be populated only by the very poor, who cannot leave, and by the automobiles of the rich who visit from the country.

The reader can protest that this presentation is loaded by adjectives like "intolerable" and by biased use of evidence, as if the country did not have its disturbances, its crime, and its hazardous weather with dangers of isolation and illness.

A partisan paragraph that admits ills in city living, but still chooses it for only one reason, its privacy, might go this way:

Almost the only thing the city offers its natives these days is anonymity, and, admittedly, a certain kind of character-building. A young woman complained the other day that in the country she could not even write her boyfriend every day because the postmistress would know and comment. But, in the city, although you may be shouldered off the pavement on the way to the post office, when you get there, your letter can be mailed without examination. It may be, even, that rigorous city living is developing the pioneer virtues as country living once did. Urban dwellers have candles and flashlights at the ready for the expected blackout. They whip out large pots and start heating up water as soon as the "hot" turns tepid, expecting an oil strike. Kerosene stoves lurk in closets for the expected chill at the turn of the seasons when landlords refuse to supply heat. Some urban dwellers are said to be growing Chinese vegetables in tubs in the cellars in expectation of the next trucking strike. Country dwellers, on the other hand, without this training in resourcefulness, are getting fat because no one walks anywhere, and pizzas, soft ice cream, and hamburger joints have invaded the rural life. They talk about culture in the country these days, but all we urban folk see is new car washes and concrete parking lots, and, in fact, the worst of the city transplanted. You country people may breathe well, and you may be developing the old urban qualities of luxury and decadence, but you can be sure that the postmistress knows about it.

DEVELOPMENT BY COMPARISON: ANALOGY

In this method of paragraph development, a second element is introduced, as it is in paragraphs developed by contrast but, the second element is an extended metaphor, as in the following paragraph: "Education today is a supermarket." And the secondary element is not truly examined for itself, but used only to illuminate the primary element—here, education:

> Some educators, brow-beaten into servility, no longer able to assert that they know their own businesses, have taken to putting aside the notion of hierarchy, the idea that some courses are more valuable than others, or that some should be taken before others and lead on to more advanced courses. Instead, they view the university as some glorious supermarket in which the consumer trundles along the aisles, taking a little marinated Russian drama, a can of instant science, and a bit of frozen English poetry. The notion is that whether the consumer chooses an intelligent diet or not he will be serving himself, happy—and, therefore, he will continue to buy at that market. Those educators who foresee the demise of Greek and Latin and are sick at what that implies about the misdirection of our presentism are termed "old guard," "rigid," and "conservative." The universities that hold to old-fashioned notions—such as, some study of foreign languages can be illuminating and some science should be required in days of space travel—are being boycotted by the self-indulgent gourmet. Education's newest idea—humanism in the variety pack or fifty-six flavors of philosophy sold in colorful, biodegradable plastic—will soon hit the shelves, and the eager supermarket managers are watching for it.

In that paragraph the supermarket analogy was used to explain the writer's objection to an idea of education in which no courses were required and the "consumer" would choose what he wished. Development by analogy does more than explain factually, of course; it can slant the material sharply according to the analogy used. The writer's contempt for this new view of education is expressed partly through the supermarket analogy. Education is accused, through the analogy, of following marketing techniques in order to obtain buyers, for greed, not in order to develop the consumer's or the student's depth of understanding. The terms "marinated," "instant," and "frozen," which carry on the analogy, suggest the distortion of the quality of Russian drama, science, and English poetry when they are compressed to be a bit of this and a dab of that. Material is "slanted" by referring to those who boycott languages and sciences, considered hard subjects, as "self-indulgent gourmets," a phrase that evokes fat, jowly, middle-aged people overeating at a banquet. The gourmets referred to may be slim, wiry, intense eighteen-year-olds, but the analogy forces the reader to consider their willfulness as self-indulgence, appropriate to eating too much of the wrong diet. The last comparison, "humanism in the variety pack" summarizes the superficiality, the artificiality, that the writer sees in education as a self-help supermarket.

That paragraph was highly partisan, angrily slanted against a certain view of education. Such slanting is one of the usual results of the extended comparison, or the paragraph development by analogy. As soon as a comparison is used, the central item gains a new or additional coloring. If the new view of education had been compared to an ocean voyage or to travel in space it would have gained qualities of wonder or curiosity or the thrill of seeing new places. If the established view of education were compared to walking through a great, ancient temple, or a gothic cathedral, or a richly paneled Elizabethan library, any one of these comparisons would have influenced the explanation of attitudes toward education. This influencing is often called "slanting" the material, predisposing the reader to react favorably or unfavorably, as the writer wishes. If the writer wishes to slant his material, he should use comparisons, because they bring to his central subject emotional qualities often very difficult to generate without them.

DEVELOPMENT THROUGH DISCUSSION:
REASONS SUPPORTING TOPIC SENTENCE

The third major kind of paragraph development is by discussion or reasoning. In these paragraphs, the meaning, the implications, or the reasoning behind the topic sentence is examined. If the topic sentence were "Sports, despite some isolated examples to the contrary, really can develop important qualities in character," the paragraph might go on to show the ways sports do provide challenges and testing grounds that develop certain qualities:

> Sports can develop important traits of personality. Although many people follow that coach who said, "Show me a good loser, and I'll show you a loser," the fact is that some sports provide the difficult moments any person needs to face alone in order to

discover that he or she can cope with them. Out hiking alone, for instance, one cannot blame someone else if he runs out of water or wears himself out by pacing himself too fast. He has to learn how to be observant and to depend on himself. He has to notice the terrain and learn how to mark trees and to use a compass in case he loses his bearings. No one wins or loses there, but a person can develop qualities of resourcefulness and self-reliance in hiking.

This "reasons" paragraph develops one central quality, self-reliance or resourcefulness, to show that sports can develop important qualities of character. The paragraph does not "prove" that sports always, or usually develop such qualities, but it states that one sport can develop these characteristics by providing the challenge and the opportunity for growth.

You might try developing reason paragraphs on a few of these topic sentences:

- People under twenty enjoy gathering in groups more than their parents do.
- The new fashions in clothes are a good sign.
- There should be a way, other than to be in the army or in college, to spend the interval between high school and adulthood.
- This country needs skilled mechanics.
- Everyone should know how to take a car's engine apart.
- Any sport or skill can develop important qualities of character.
- Basketball is a great sport.

Those topic sentences seem to suggest development by reasons, illustrations, or a combination of both methods. Determine which method will be most effective for each topic sentence and use it to develop the paragraph.

DEVELOPMENT BY DISCUSSION: CAUSE AND EFFECT

In this type of paragraph development the topic sentence expresses the cause and the rest of the paragraph describes effects stemming from that cause. "When William, the eldest son, became a forest ranger and went off to Maine, the family fell apart." Clearly, that topic sentence is aimed for development by effects. Write that paragraph yourself. How did the family depend on William, and how did his leaving affect them? It almost writes itself. You might try writing a paragraph or two growing out of these topic sentences:

- The automobile has transformed American living.
- Learning carpentry led the whole class into new activities.
- When he first heard about the moon landing, he did not believe it.
- The rock festival affected the whole town.

Starting from the following vague topics, write your own topic sentences for cause-and-effect paragraphs: television, a new job, marks, money pressures on a family, alcoholism, parades, writing for a magazine.

DEVELOPMENT BY DISCUSSION: EFFECT AND SUGGESTED CAUSES

Although we know that social conditions exist, usually we do not really know their cause or causes. For this reason, the effect/causes paragraph is primarily conjectural; it discusses probable or suggested causes. What accounts for the recent rise in the crime rate in suburbia? (The crime rate is the effect.) The writer develops the paragraph, suggesting the causes he can see in order of increasing interest as usual:

- Better reporting of crime (not necessarily more crime).
- Congestion in suburbs.
- Easy access to houses.
- Easy access to highways out of the area.
- Lack of jobs and training for jobs.
- Lack of future hopes.
- Rise in drug addiction.

Paragraphs built on this model can lead to unsupported generalizations, the most common error of "deep think" pieces, but if the causes are presented as some, not all, and probable, not sole, the paragraphs can be interesting and useful. The narrower the topic, the greater your chances are to avoid being vague and windy in overgeneralizing. The excellent state of the paint job you did has a number of specific causes that you know about: good brushes, good paint, attention to detail, and, of course, your skill.

DEVELOPMENT BY DISCUSSION: DEFINITION

Frequently in an essay the writer needs to pause to discuss a word or concept because the rest of his essay depends upon the audience's understanding of his use of the term. In the following paragraph a definition of "realism" is set within a discussion of larger movements:

> **Neoclassicism** and **romanticism,** then, are large and loose terms, referring to movements that have both a common literary theory and practice, and a more or less coherent world view. Other movements are somewhat more restricted. **Realism,** for example, is primarily a matter of technique. It aims at giving an authentic picture of ordinary life, usually by showing typical people of the middle and lower classes engaged in ordinary pursuits, and by recording their activities in great and concrete detail. In novels of the eighteenth and nineteenth centuries, particularly those of Defoe and Balzac and Howells, great emphasis is given to seemingly inconsequential people, who are portrayed in a rigorously unidealized way, and to such externals as the sights and sounds of common life. We are so accustomed to the technique that we now tend to take it for granted, especially in the novel, but when Tolstoy's contemporaries read in *War and Peace* about Pierre's suddenly becoming conscious of the creaking of Princess Hélène's corset, many were startled and dismayed by the intimate realistic detail. When attention is paid not only to externals but also to the intricate workings of the mind, as it is in the subtle and detailed characterizations of Henry James, the term **psychological realism** is used.[5]

Notice the transitional links, "Neoclassicism and romanticism, then, . . . Other movements are somewhat more restricted. Realism, for example, . . ." Focus is firmly placed on realism, a "more restricted" movement, in contrast with the larger, looser terms defined earlier.

Frequently the writer may have to define a word or a term using its dictionary meaning, its etymology or history as a word, and its repeated use in one context. (A context can be one text, such as the Bill of Rights, one novel, or a selection of works by one writer.

It is any grouping that may be considered, by some rational principle, unified.) In the following passage of definition, the author defines Shakespeare's use of the word "fool" in certain sonnets:

> Here and elsewhere in the Sonnets the fool is one who has been made a fool of (by Love or Time), who is somebody's or something's dupe or sport: "Love's not Time's fool" (116); "the fools of Time" (124); "Thou blind fool, Love, what dost thou to mine eyes./That they behold and see not what they see?" (137). On the most obvious level, then, the speaker qualifies as a fool because he is "stupid" enough to be duped by love, which is traditionally blind. He is also a servant or slave, a talker, and a condoner of sin, roles which further entitle him to be called "fool.". . . "Fool" derives from a Latin word for "bellows," which in late Latin became "windbag, fool" and a number of passages in Proverbs and Ecclesiastes remind us that a "fool . . . is full of words." In the Bible "fool" often signifies "sinner," a sense that fits the poet to the extent that he sins in condoning "ill," corrupting himself by salving the friend's "amiss". . . .[6]

This paragraph of definition discusses Shakespeare's interpretation of the word "fool." It mentions three sonnets (116, 124, 137) that use the word in the obvious sense, " 'stupid' enough to be duped by love." It defines fool in four other senses and draws upon etymology and scripture as well. In paragraphs of definition, then, remember that a word has its dictionary meaning, its denotation, but it has also the meaning that it gains from usage, from its appearance in many contexts. Yet, for you as writer its most important context is its use by the author you are discussing.

DEVELOPMENT BY DISCUSSION: DEFINITION AND LIMITATION, NEGATIVE AND POSITIVE

Definition paragraphs, so common and so important to nonfiction often have to include statements of limitation. In treating, for example, "love of country," you may wish to include the immigrant's love of his new land, but wish to exclude love of the countryside. A paragraph that defined, qualified, and limited the scope of your term "love of country" would be helpful. In treating the term "revolution," Bayard Rustin states in the first paragraph of "The Failure of Black Separatism" that the term is much overused. The third paragraph begins with this sentence: "There has been, it is true, some moderate improvement in the economic condition of Negroes, but by no stretch of the imagination could it be called revolutionary." See the way he works up to that sentence:

We are living in an age of revolution—or so they tell us. The children of the affluent classes pay homage to their parents' values by rejecting them; this, they say, is a youth revolution. The discussion and display of sexuality increases—actors disrobe on stage, young women very nearly do on the street—and so we are in the midst of a sexual revolution. Tastes in music and clothing change, and each new fashion too is revolutionary. With every new social phenomenon now being dubbed a "revolution," the term has in fact become nothing more than a slogan which serves to take our minds off an unpleasant reality. For if we were not careful, we might easily forget that there is a conservative in the White House, that our country is racially polarized as never before, and that the forces of liberalism are in disarray. Whatever there is of revolution today, in any meaningful sense of the term, is coming from the Right.

But we are also told—and with far greater urgency and frequency—that there is a black revolution. If by revolution we mean a radical escalation of black aspirations and demands, this is surely the case. There is a new assertion of pride in the Negro race and its cultural heritage, and although the past summer was marked by the lack of any major disruptions, there is among blacks a tendency more pronounced than at any time in Negro history to engage in violence and the rhetoric of violence. Yet if we look closely at the situation of Negroes today, we find that there has been not the least revolutionary reallocation of political or economic power. There is, to be sure, an increase in the number of black elected officials throughout the United States and particularly in the South, but this has largely been the result of the 1965 Voting Rights act, which was passed before the "revolution". . . . Some reallocation of political power has indeed taken place since the Presidential election of 1964, but generally its beneficiaries have been the Republicans and the anti-Negro forces. Nor does this particular trend show much sign of abating. . . . Moreover. . . . And if the Democrats only break even in 1970, the Republicans will control the Senate for the first time since 1954. A major defeat would leave the Democrats weaker than they have been at any time since the conservative days of the 1920s.

There has been, it is true, some moderate improvement in

96

the economic condition of Negroes, but by no stretch of the imagination could it be called revolutionary.[7]

Rustin's problem was to assert firmly that "moderate improvement" did exist, but that this should not, according to his thinking, be given the term "revolutionary."

Is There Any Particular Problem about Writing the Paragraph of Definition and Qualification?

Transitions and modifying links have to hold the writer's attitudes clear for the reader to grasp his emphasis. If Rustin had been saying, "You bet there's a revolution. Look at this. . . . Look at that. . . . And then there is this . . . and don't forget that change," the reader could settle back and let his mind gallop on but Rustin's idea was more complex than that. First, he wanted to point out that the word "revolution" is so debased that Americans use it for trivial shifts in taste. Then, he had to agree that some tendencies are indeed important and new, but they have not led to significant reallocations of power. Again, he had to grant that there had been some power shifts, but he observed that they did not serve Negroes predominantly. That is, the author was threading his way through complexities, trying to set his emphasis just where he wanted it. "But we are told . . . . if by revolution we mean . . . this is surely the case. There is . . . and although . . . there is . . . . Yet . . . we find . . . . There is, to be sure . . . but this has largely been . . . . Some . . . but . . . ." One can go through the second paragraph observing his granting—"There is," and "to be sure"—and his taking away—"but," "yet," and "although." Transitional links are useful, even vital, to all smoothly moving prose, but nowhere more crucial than in paragraphs of definition and qualification.

DEVELOPMENT BY DISCUSSION: DEFINITION BY NEGATIVE ASSERTION

There is yet another kind of definition paragraph that can be useful to the student: the definition by negative assertion. Suppose Rustin had begun his paragraph saying, "A revolution is not a mere shift in values in which children oppose their parents' notions of decorum. Shifts in taste leading the young to wear denims and beads do not signify any power shift important enough to be called 'revolutionary.' " He might move along asserting repeatedly what a revolution is not until he came to state firmly that anything important enough to be termed revolutionary would involve a significant shift of power to a group that had not held power before. He would then assert that Negroes had not been the beneficiaries of any such reallocation, although they had achieved some moderate gains. In that sense, then, the term "revolution" could not apply to the life of blacks in America.

As a gardener removes weeds until the plant stands clear, the writer can eliminate what he does <u>not</u> mean in order to clarify what he <u>does</u> mean. Yet, if he wishes, he can use the rejected ideas to define his meaning; he does not have to consider them valueless. For example:

> **If by revolution we mean some radical change, any change, some people would say that we are in the midst of a revolution in fashions. But since a true revolution has some permanence and fashions will follow one another as fast as designers can sketch them, we can hardly dignify the newest fashion in dress by the term revolution. They are fads, nothing more.**

In that way, as the writer rejects fashion as unrevolutionary, he works to define his own use of the word "revolution." You might try to define some abstract terms, like "friendship" ("loyalty," "prayer," "patriotism," "sensitivity," "tolerance"), using development by negative assertion. "Friendship is not . . . ." Comparisons and contrasts might be useful in your paragraph, too.

SUMMARY OF TYPES OF PARAGRAPH DEVELOPMENT

As you consider all of these ways of developing paragraphs—through amplification (one illustration, several illustrations, restatement, classification), through introduction of a second important element (comparison, contrast, analogy), through discussion (reasons that support the topic sentence, effects of the topic sentence, causes of an effect or condition, definition and limitation of important terms, definition by negative assertions)—it should be clear that often more than one of these methods is used in one paragraph. Moreover, the problem determines the writer's method, not vice versa. That is, you, as writer, choose the method of paragraph development that will serve your purpose best.

What If the Writer Unknowingly Mixes Methods of Development in One Paragraph?

The more conscious the writer is of the methods he uses, the better, of course, but he may combine methods of paragraph development intentionally or without knowing that he does. Most paragraphs do employ more than one technique of development. If a writer should swing from one method of development to another, there is no reason to object, provided that his logical line of argument remains clear. After introducing himself to this variety of techniques, the young writer can notice methods of paragraph development that he reads in fiction and nonfiction. He can select his own techniques more consciously than before, but always he will see that in nonfiction the same formula—topic and support—is at work. Even as he tells his classmates why he prefers travel by bus to hitchhiking, he will be developing a spoken paragraph by contrast and by definition and qualification. He will be supporting his "main idea" by the technique that works.

transitions

How Do the Professionals Make Their Writing Smooth?

It is true that the biggest difference between the writing of professionals and the writing of students, if both are correct and articulate, seems to be smoothness. In actuality, a paragraph can seem very smooth and say close to nothing; smoothness is not necessarily an index of high quality of thought. Skillful use of transitional tags can conceal large gaps in thought. But, in the main, there are probably two factors responsible for the smoothness we all admire in professional writing: the logical ordering of sentences and the use of transitions.

Without ordering the reasons, and without providing any transitions, list all the reasons you can think of in support of the topic sentence: "Private cars should be banned from the cities." The reasons set up as a paragraph might go something like this:

Private cars should be banned from the city. Cars cause pollution. Numbers of cars parked in the streets slow down traffic. The parked cars prevent business from being transacted easily. They cause congestion. There is danger to pedestrians. The bad air is a danger to everybody, particularly old people and children. Parking cars in the streets instead of in garages leads to car thefts. The car-theft rings lead to increased criminal activity of all sorts.

Now, number the sentences in order of their increasing importance. (A choice of priorities is involved there.) How will the paragraph look with changes in sentence order? Try this:

- Private cars should be banned from the city.
- Cars cause congestion.
- Numbers of cars parked in the streets slow down traffic.
- They prevent business from being transacted easily.
- They lead to car thefts.
- The car-theft rings lead to increased criminal activity in cities.
- There is danger to pedestrians. (From parked cars? This needs to be fixed.)
- They cause pollution.
- The bad air is a danger to everybody.
- Old people, ill people, and children suffer most from the bad air.

The logical ordering helped some. The passage is not smooth yet, but it is getting smoother. As you read that skeleton paragraph you may notice that the pattern of sentences is repetitive. Most of the sentences have the pattern of subject-verb. The addition of transitional words will help to smooth out the passage, but the sentence patterns will still need some work:

Private cars should be banned from the city. In the first place, they cause congestion. The sheer number of parked cars in the streets slows down traffic. Slow traffic can prevent business from being transacted easily. But, of course, there is a rise in one kind of business, car thefts. The numbers of parked cars are an invitation to rings of car thieves and thus to increased activities of gangsters in the cities. These numbers of cars add inevitably to pollution of the air, which adds to hazardous and unpleasant living conditions, not just for the active pedestrian sprinting across the street against the light, but for the older person, for the ill, or for children who have to breathe the noxious exhaust fumes (Don't the active people have to breathe them? This has to be fixed.)

The transitional phrases "in the first place," "but, of course" and repetitions like "the sheer number," "the numbers," "these numbers" helped, but the paragraph ends in the air, polluted air at that, and the whole thing does not seem to hang together yet. The first two sentences seem all right as they are. Are there small bits that you might add to enliven the paragraph? It seems so predictable. The rings of car thieves add color, but at the moment they do not seem major reasons to ban cars from the cities. Isn't that like banning matches because some people light fire to themselves? The abuse of a good thing never has been an important reason to abolish it. Is there some general idea that all of this might work toward?

Try the paragraph again, working to "fill in" with informative details and to work toward some unifying idea—the importance of human comfort, for instance:

> Private cars should be banned from the city. Unquestionably, many people enjoy the freedom they offer, but they do increase congestion. The sheer numbers of parked cars—waiting for owners to use them on Friday evening—slow down weekday traffic. Private cars parked on the street force delivery trucks to double-park as they make deliveries. The cross streets, made for four-lane traffic, slow taxis to a one-lane creep. I have read that traffic in New York City moves cross-town today three miles an hour slower than in the days of horse and buggy. Consider just the effect of that slow traffic on business activity! Although business has always been centered in the cities, when business becomes increasingly difficult it moves elsewhere. In addition, thanks to the car, cities are becoming increasingly intolerable for simple human living. Pollution, not to mention the hazards for pedestrians dodging traffic across wide streets, makes cities unpleasant and even dangerous for many, particularly the elderly, the handicapped, and the young. There are other unpleasant effects. Those lines of parked, seldom-used cars invite car thieves, whose individual success feeds into the flourishing network of car-theft rings. This, in turn, contributes to the dangerous rise in criminal activities of other sorts. You might argue that the rise in car thefts is hardly a reason to ban the car, that we should, instead, ban the thieves, and as a car owner, I would agree. But when we consider all the unpleasant ways in which private cars in the cities affect our lives and our work, perhaps we should ban the thieves, as well as congestion and pollution, by banning the private car.

If it seems that a lot of filling in came from nowhere and changed this paragraph beyond recognition, try this same exercise in reverse. Here is a brief passage from an article written by Diana Trilling, about Norman Mailer:

> Naturally enough, of the various excesses into which Mailer is led by his own option against civilization, the most disturbing is his expressed tolerance of, even his partisanship with, extreme personal violence. And he is not speaking metaphorically; here as elsewhere he is announcing a program of action. What is worse, he speaks of violence in a language of love learned in the moral culture he undertakes to dismiss in its entirety. For example, in a statement which he made in the course of an interview in *Mademoiselle* (February 1961), he has this to say about a brutal gratuitous murder. . . ."[8]

If you listed the major points of that passage they would be:

- Mailer opposes civilization.
- He approves of personal violence.
- He means it, as a course of action.
- He speaks of violence in a language of love.
- He gives evidence of this outlook in an interview.

Transitional phrases smoothed out the material: "Naturally enough," "the most disturbing," "even his partisanship with," "and," "here as elsewhere," "what is worse," "for example." Each sentence, in other words, had at least one transitional element, many of which expressed logical relationships between sentence elements.

The writer seems to have thought something like this:

Mailer opposes civilization.
His approval of personal violence is an expression of that view.
Nor is that expression just metaphorical; he means it as a program of action.
He somehow makes it worse by speaking of violence in the language of love, a language learned in the culture he tries to dismiss.
Give that example from the interview.

For practice in constructing transitions, you might try one or two of these exercises.

- Select a paragraph from a magazine or from the editorial page of a local paper. List the main point of each sentence without including its transitional words. Does it move from least important to most important item? Would you wish to reverse or alter its order of importance?
- Select one of these "Proverbs of Hell" from William Blake's *Marriage of Heaven and Hell*. List the main ideas that you might present in your paragraph on his aphorism. Arrange them in order of increasing importance and then present them in a formal paragraph using transitional words and phrases to relate your points logically to one another. By the way, these will be, probably, discussion paragraphs built on the "reasons" model: topic sentence and reasons in support of topic sentence.

- A fool sees not the same tree that a wise man sees.
- Shame is Pride's Cloak.
- Prisons are built with stones of Law, Brothels with bricks of Religion.
- Always be ready to speak your mind, and a base man will avoid you.
- He who has suffered you to impose on him knows you.
- Expect poison from the standing water.
- If the lion was advised by the fox, he would be cunning.
- The crow wished that every thing was black, the owl, that everything was white.[9]

How Does the Paper, as a Whole, Move Toward its Conclusion?

The paper uses, primarily, the same transitional devices between paragraphs as it does within the individual paragraph. Ideas appear in order of increasing importance, and to smooth over the linking between them, transition phrases and words express their logical relationships. The central difference between transitions that link sentences and those that link paragraphs is merely the size of the segment. The sequence of sentences expresses the series of related ideas within the paragraphs, and the sequence of paragraphs expresses the order of ideas in the paper as a whole. The transitional words and phrases between paragraphs and between sentences are the same: words indicating agreement, like "and," "another," "moreover," "furthermore," "indeed"; and words indicating contrast, like "however," "but," "on the other hand," "still."

As you read magazines and newspapers, begin to watch the transitional elements used between paragraphs. To return for a moment to the paragraph banning private cars from cities: "But when we consider all the unpleasant ways in which private cars in the cities affect our lives and our work, perhaps we should ban the thieves, as well as congestion and pollution, by banning the private car." That sentence is constructed to review the paragraph's central ideas, to set those ideas (congestion and pollution) in relation to a larger idea (unpleasant effect on life and work), and to thump on its main point (banning private cars) at the end of the sentence, the point of greatest effect. Suppose that paragraph were part of a larger essay discussing the state of the cities, how could the writer move away from such a thumping conclusion? He needs an equally emphatic transition beginning his next paragraph. He might say something like this: "This change, important as it is, should not be contemplated without a radical improvement in mass transportation. If we banned the car without improving the means to move those hoards of people who live and work in the city, our lungs would be wonderfully healthy, but we would have no food."

"This change" restates the subject, banning the private car; "important as it is" concedes the value of the point that will be opposed before the sentence moves on to its main idea. The second sentence expands upon two matters: what mass transportation specifically refers to—the moving of individuals who live and work in the city (and incidentally, this pulls the concrete out of the abstraction "mass transportation"); and why mass transportation is vital—that it provides a way for people to get their food by providing a way to work.

Is the Idea, Then, to Sprinkle Transitional Words Around to Remind the Reader of the Subject?

Partly, that is true. "This change," in the example given above, reminds the reader of the subject, but it is a mistake to think of transitional words and phrases as tags, bits sprinkled here or there to make things look linked up. That kind of cleverness can introduce fakery into your writing. Try to aim for a smoothness that is based on tight, logical relationships. The transitional words express a logical relationship, and their value should not be underrated as "merely verbal."

Often in thinking of transitions as "just tags," writers mistake the additive for the causal. For example, they will begin a paragraph by saying, "The second quality that. . . ." The transitional element there is "second," but the actual relation may not be "another" of two or three. If the "quality" is an outgrowth of the first one, or subordinate to it, or caused by it, then, "the second quality" does not express its actual logical relationship, which is causal, not additional. Young writers often think of their composition as composed of equal paragraphs. But paragraphs may be equal in length or importance and still express ideas that cannot be joined by transitional words expressing the additive relation, like "second," "third," "fourth," or "in addition" or "similarly." For example, it would obscure the relation between the two needs to begin that second paragraph with "Similarly, the cities need an intense campaign to improve mass transportation." The relationship is not that the cities need to improve mass transportation also; they need it first, or banning the private car might cause terrible problems such as loss of jobs; "should not be contemplated without a radical improvement" expressed the actual relationship between the two problems, which "moreover" or "similarly" would not have done.

Notice the way Mary Bunyea, a freshman, handled the transitions in the following paragraph. She was given a problem: to write a paragraph with the topic sentence "Americans must adopt a more sensible attitude toward pollution." Then the class decided what points all paragraphs should contain: health reasons, ruining of land, effect on man, killing of wildlife, and pollution of beaches. From that jumble, the class tried to put the ideas into logical order and write in any needed transitions.

> Americans must adopt a more sensible attitude toward pollution. They must take a good long look at the effects of pollution on all forms of life and nature. They must realize that pollution has ruined our land and destroyed our beaches, rivers, lakes and ponds. Sewage and garbage are poured into our waters day after day, ton after ton. Millions of trees are cut down so the land can be "developed" for the sake of industrialization and expansion.

Consequently, the fumes and waste products that industries let flow into the air and water have driven away and killed much of our wild life. And not only are animals being hurt by pollution, but man is also finding that his own health is endangered. So, in effect, if they are to survive in this world and interact with nature as man should, Americans must face the responsibilities of environmental conservation and protection for his own sake.

——Mary Bunyea

Every sentence in that tight paragraph has a word or phrase that refers to the idea of the previous sentence or suggests the logical continuity between two sentences. The second and the third sentences repeat in "they" and "pollution" the basic idea of the topic sentence. Sentences 4 and 5 repeat by examples the way pollution is ruining the land. "Consequently," "and not only . . . but" "so, in effect" express genuine logical relationships carried out in the sentences, not just apparent or verbal connections.

Underline the transitional words and phrases you find in this student's paragraph:

Life seemingly holds more excitement for more people than ever before in history. Yet, the very air we breathe presents a major problem to men. And the waters we depend upon for drinking, for agriculture, and for recreation are clouded with pollutants which can cause great harm. Furthermore, another problem is the disposal of waste. From the discards of our productive technology, we are faced with a crisis in our environment. On the other hand, with modern technology, we can reduce pollution in our environment. We no longer need to contaminate the winds that blow through cities with such great volumes of foul gas from our vehicles, factories, and homes as we do now. By using electrical power and modern means of refuse disposal, we could lessen the city's pollution of the earth's atmosphere. Moreover, we could also reduce the contamination of water. Chemical and mechanical engineers are capable of improving both the input and output lines in ways that would help the whole country get more use and pleasure from its water resources. Lastly, most of the bottles and boxes that contain our food cannot be compacted or consumed when emptied. The producers of nonreturnable and nondegrading containers could quickly find substitutes in which to place their products. As a result, the problem of pollution could be on its way to be solved.

——Barbara Otremba

What Can a Writer Do if He Cannot Find a Logical Link Between Paragraphs?

If he cannot find one there is something wrong. Two paragraphs set next to one another within a larger essay must have some reason for being in that order. Usually they are trotting along, each doing its modest share to demonstrate the vivid truth of the author's thesis. The first paragraph should be leading on to the second. The writer who is stuck for a transition needs to ask himself what the central idea of each of the paragraphs is. How does paragraph *A* relate to or connect with paragraph *B?* Often the logical connection is there and was the reason that the writer put the paragraph where he did in the first place. Usually, all the writer has to do is to make explicit (to "say out") that logical connection he knew all the time.

There is, however, the possibility that there is no logical relation between two contiguous paragraphs and that one of them should be moved elsewhere in the paper. Once the writer thinks of that possibility, he often sees immediately where the paragraph can be truly effective and sees that he was wasting its force in the old location, because the ideas could not move freely forward in their next logical step. Some writers think, "And recopy all that, just to move a paragraph?" Indeed, recopy, but that is the main reason for counting on a rough draft and at least one revision. Expect to rearrange and recopy paragraphs, and be glad if only one or two are out of place.

Now it should be clear that transitions are far from insignificant or mere verbal tags; they are expressions of the paper's inherent logic and, therefore, should be part of the paper's planning from the earliest stage of organization. At that early moment when you begin to sort your notes, you are thinking about your "biggest ideas." Then identify your main ideas and plan their sequence. At that time, you should be considering transitions, ways to move between big ideas. First, try to set your ideas so close to one another, in such tight logical relationships, that there is very little mental distance between them. When that is possible, little more than a word or two is needed in transition between paragraphs. At times you will want to pick up the reader bodily and move him by saying something like, "Considered from another angle." But that kind of hoist and heave transition should be used only if it is truly necessary to move the whole machinery around to another angle. Perhaps that other angle is a part of something already under discussion. Generally speaking, plan so that you can confine your transition to brief words of restatement or logical connection like "therefore," "nevertheless," and "however." Hope to keep "Not only is . . . but also" to a minimum.

But Why Are Transitions so Important Anyway? What Difference Does a Logical Connection Make?

Transitions keep the reader's mind following the writer's thought closely and prevent him from drifting off. They make reading seem easy by nudging the reader with the logical link, so that he does not have to ask himself why an idea is being presented at this point and not another. A marvelous idea can go unobserved if the writer is not there with the comment that says, in effect, "We have been talking about this all along. This is easy." It must be admitted that even the energetic reader can be distracted or predisposed to dislike the writer's main idea if it is opposed to his own philosophy. Transitions can help there too, by insisting on the logical, rational connections so that the reader is persuaded to accept the logic of the argument. Finally, transitions affect tone as well as logic. Casual links like "it is true that," "partly," or "some people say" give an informal, relaxed tone to a passage. "Nonetheless," "furthermore," or "on the contrary" suggest a more formal tone. Each mode is appropriate in particular circumstances. Contributing to the tone of the essay is one more service performed by the transition word or phrase.

The overwhelming purpose of the transition is to set and hold the logical sequence so clearly that the paragraphs seem to race toward the essay's conclusion. The reader never has to stop and ask himself, "Where am I?" or "How did I get here?" He knows where he is because the transitions are there telling him in almost every sentence. Transitions help keep the pace of the work brisk; they aid in holding the reader's interest by helping him to follow the author's mental line or argument, and best of all, they keep the muddle out. They keep the writer's thinking squarely before the mind of the reader so that he must follow and be persuaded, or admit that he fell off the rails somewhere through his own perversity.

109

conclusions

How Should I Write a Conclusion?

Instead, ask the question asked about the introduction: "What does the conclusion do?" Is it to be understood as the paper's ending paragraphs or the conclusion of the subject? Is it expected to conclude all further consideration of a particular topic, to bring some "new light of wisdom" on a subject long considered by graybeards? Isn't that too much to expect from almost anyone?

To be well aimed, a conclusion must be understood as the paper's conclusion, its terminating and summary paragraph—definitely not the conclusion of the subject. Granted, it is the writer's best thought at the time of writing, but it cannot purport to be definitive, for the writer himself should expect to grow and so better in six months. The conclusion should merely review or restate the paper's main points, preferably in order of increasing importance. It need not do more than that to be sound and effective.

Just a word on the mystery conclusion, a particular type of ending paragraph that some students aim for, but that most professionals avoid. According to the mystery conclusion the paper is a kind of detective story in which the writer piles up evidence toward a solution. Then, when the heap of evidence has grown to pyramid size, the writer-magician plans to whirl his red handkerchief and, in a brilliant concluding two or three paragraphs, to solve the mystery. Such a conclusion is exceedingly difficult to manage, and if it fails, the paper is a shambles, because the writer has deliberately withheld clues in order to bring flashing clarity with his triumphant concluding paragraph. The central confusion here is the term "conclusion," which many students take to mean "solution," end of a mystery, and not merely a clear paragraph that summarizes the writer's main points.

How Can I Be Sure to Restate the Paper's Main Points?

Reread the paper, noting the topic sentence of each paragraph. Consider the paper's main segments, and be sure that their main ideas are mentioned again in the conclusion. Reread the introduction to be sure that its main ideas have been covered by the conclusion (and that no basic point in the conclusion is omitted by the introduction). The most difficult problem of the conclusion is not in restating the paper's main points, but in doing so interestingly with grace.

If the Conclusion Just Restates the Old Points, How Can It Be Interesting?

Watch the professionals. Notice the way journalists and professional scholars manage to make restatement of the old ideas fresh and entertaining. Often they recall or echo an earlier idea, image, or comparison and, by using it, recall the earlier thought, to bring the essay back full circle. The circular form somehow is pleasing to the mind of the reader; it gives a kind of closure and finish to the essay.

Fischer's essay "War as theater of the absurd" (see p. 76) consisted mainly of episodes demonstrating the zaniness of war as illustrated in a volume he had received from the Pentagon. The last sentence of his second paragraph, the conventional position for a statement of an essay's subject and thesis, said this: "More often they seemed downright zany, like scenes stolen from the theater of the absurd." His essay's concluding sentence recalled that allusion: "Whenever I remember the story these days, I can't help thinking what a lovely script it would have made for the Marquis de Sade and his company of actors in the Charenton asylum."[10]

In citing the very origin of much of the current interest in "theater of the absurd" mentioned in his title, Fischer wrapped the matter up neatly. In academic research papers, the mere mention of a central image can not do all the work of the conclusion. Nor is this sufficient for many of Fischer's more complex presentations of issues and ideas, and at the close of those more formal expositions, Fischer uses a fuller, more specifically enumerative conclusion. There is not one conclusion for journalistic writing and another for so-called academic writing. They share the same model for the basic conclusion, but more variation of this pattern is permitted journalists, who will, when necessary, write the denser, more thorough conclusion often described as "academic."

Sometimes a good quotation from a critic can be useful to refresh the conclusion, although the quotation should be brief and should not seem too artificially set. It is better, on the whole, to tuck that quotation within the concluding paragraph of restatement and to end on your own words. Sometimes the professionals will end, after reviewing the main points of the article, on a vignette, a very short story, that illustrates the main points they have been making all along. Essentially, they take their globe of facts, ideas, and opinions and turn it slightly just so the light strikes it differently, and the conclusion seems fresh, although not one idea in it is actually new.

Although in general, no idea in the conclusion is expected to be new, it is necessary to repeat the old ones, particularly if the paper is long, because the reader may have forgotten the points that were made earlier. Moreover, points mentioned all at once in the swing of their logical series sometimes can be seen and understood better because they are seen in relation to one another instead of being widely separated through the paper. In the paper each idea is treated and supported with particular relation to the material immediately around it. In the conclusion, the direct relations of the ideas to one another can be stark and clear, perhaps for the first time. That presentation is, in itself, new, and bears an emphasis.

What Should Be the Manner or Tone of the Conclusion?

Should the writer aim for a quiet conclusion or one that ends his paper with a roll of drums and a flourish of trumpets? The solution to that problem depends upon three main elements: the subject, the audience, and the writer's own manner adopted throughout the paper. Many teachers say that this is the writer's last chance to make his point with emphasis. They say that he should speak now, emphatically, and raise his voice a bit louder. It is true that in the last sentences the writer must make quite certain that the main idea he has been asserting is utterly clear to the reader and viewed in its most favorable and persuasive perspective. But what is the way for this particular writer to gain the most persuasive perspective on this subject with this audience?

Is this audience one that enjoys being carried on a rising wave of righteous indignation? That may be good for the circulation, but it would appeal mainly to a fairly naïve audience. Does the author feel comfortable asserting that his way is right, as he carries the banner of hope forward into the future? You could feel odd, vehemently asserting a cliché like that. Is the subject so clear that vehemence is appropriate? If, for example, the cafeteria obviously needs reform, the reforms are practical, economical, and just await someone's energy, then by all means work up a good head of steam and blast the stagnant apathy out of the room. The main thing is to determine, judiciously, your manner of closing.

Sometimes it helps to ask yourself, "What kind of a conclusion would I want to read at the end of this paper?" Would you want to feel that without actions that you recommend humankind is going straight to the pit of disaster? Or do you want to suggest that, although life is difficult, with some good judgment and sanity—which involves, of course, following the recommendations made in your paper—there is some hope? Are you aiming for a slight upbeat at the end of a vigorous paper? Or a serious statement of warning at the end of a paper that, despite its serious intentions, has been fairly light in tone throughout? There are many shades in atmosphere and feeling, of course. The conclusion needs to be definite and clear in its meaning, but its feeling or tone, can be anywhere on a long spectrum of moods. Your choice depends upon your own judgment of what will predispose your reader to consider your suggestions favorably.

It is important, for instance, not to mistake your own pleasure at this chance to speak your mind with your reader's pleasure at hearing you. You may feel release at this glorious chance to say what you think of the Governor or the President, but unless you know your reader feels as you do, you may turn him away by the fierceness of your indignation. Since sincerity of emotion has never been an accurate measure of either justice or wisdom, many people fear the zealot. But many people are delighted by the impassioned rousing speech, feeling, "At last, someone feels intensely, as I do." Writers, then, need to imagine their audiences. If they are lucky, people who do not agree with them will read their work. Usually, we all speak to a small circle of friends and pass back and forth ideas that we all agree with anyway. But to communicate seriously, sequentially, and perhaps persuasively with the antagonistic stranger who might be led to agree is an opportunity not to be lost in self-indulgent venting of righteous indignation.

Why Can't I Just Speak My Mind and Summarize the Paper's Main Points?

The best conclusion, and potentially perhaps the most persuasive one, is the restatement of the paper's main ideas in a moderate but definite and clear fashion. If the writer wants primarily the release of self-expression, he will choose to speak his mind and, to vary Blake, let the base man avoid him. But if he wants primarily to influence his audience, genuinely to try to reform conditions, he will speak with conviction, yes, but also with the understanding that his opposers are not necessarily "base" and that they might—just might—be persuaded if they understood more thoroughly.

Is All Writing This Calculated— Even Dishonest?

All writing is calculated. If you write in your room alone at night, you are writing for some reason, to portray something to someone. You may be writing to make sense of some emotional tangle just for yourself, but still your writing has an aim. In order to achieve this aim, you select certain words. If your aim is to state the truth as clearly as you see it, you will choose certain words. If your aim is to persuade others of the truth of your statements, then awareness of individual reactions must enter into your selection process. Then you cannot state the truth as baldly as you see it, or think you see it, because stated thus it might be rejected for irrelevant reasons as untrue—too complex, too simple, too ugly, too unkind, too vulgar—too something. Weighing the possibility of rejection, for a trivial, irrational, or irrelevant cause against the importance of your convictions, you may choose to say what you think differently. That is calculation, and to the extent that it produces writing that is not the direct outpouring of anger, horror, grief, insult, or whatever you might express to a friend who is predisposed to accept and agree, it is dishonest.

It is a strange idea that equates honesty only with spontaneity and rarely with determined and deliberate decision. If a young writer does equate only spontaneity with honesty, then, because all writing is calculated, it is a dishonest medium. But is honesty only blurted out? Can one not decide deliberately to be honest? If the writer recognizes that words cannot be "natural" and, in some wacky surrealistic fashion, grow out of his mouth like a vine, then he must agree that speaking and writing both involve conscious selection of words. As he arranges idea sequences, so he selects words. He is, in fact, quite stuck with the responsibility of his conscious, careful choice of both words and ideas in sequence. He has a difficult range of choices: he can say nothing; he can say anything; or he can choose what he says.

NOTES FOR PART 2

1. Otto Friedrich, "Reunion in Concord," *Harper's,* May 1971, p. 87.

2. John Fischer, "The Easy Chair: War as Theater of the Absurd," *Harper's,* March 1970, p. 18.

3. John Hollow, "William Morris and the Judgment of God," *PMLA,* 86 (1971), 446.

4. Elaine Showalter, "Women and the Literary Curriculum," *College English,* 32 (1971), 855.

5. Marlies K. Danziger and W. Stacy Johnson, *An Introduction to the Study of Literature* (Boston, Mass.: D. C. Heath, and Company, 1965), p. 122.

6. Hilton Landry, *Interpretations in Shakespeare's Sonnets* (Berkeley: Univ. of California Press, 1963), p. 77.

7. Bayard Rustin, "The Failure of Black Separatism," *Harper's,* Jan. 1970, p. 25.

8. Diana Trilling, "The Radical Moralism of Norman Mailer," in *The Creative Present,* ed. Nona Balakian and Charles Simmons (New York: Doubleday, 1963), pp. 167–68.

9. William Blake, "Proverbs of Hell," in *The Marriage of Heaven and Hell* (London: J. M. Dent and Sons, 1927), pp. 7–10. [Spelling and punctuation has been modernized.]

10. Fischer, pp. 18, 29.

preparation
of the
paper

finding a subject

What Should I Write About?

Whenever an essay is assigned in school or college in any class from sociology to English, students worry, "What should I write about?" The "should" needs to be taken from the question. That question, so often asked, is actually two questions disguised: "What is there to write about?" and "What do I want to think and learn about?"

There is, literally, everything to write about. No subject is unworthy of writing or, many people believe, of art. Matters that you might consider insignificant—what it feels like to return to your old hometown, a discussion of an author's early girl friends, a character portrayal of a parent, what it was like for a successful writer to go back to college in his middle age—all of these have been the central topics of recent articles in *Harper's Magazine*. Any one of these topics might have been discounted as boring if assigned in an English class, but lively articles have been written about them. First, then, follow your own interest and push at a topic a bit, turning it this way and that, to see where your own angle on a subject catches the light.

Take a general subject like music. Are you interested in the physics behind the sounding of notes, the development of rock, the relation of the harpsichord to the piano, the current bootlegging of the works of popular musicians, the story of the blues? Any topic is fascinating as soon as you begin to think about it, but most people draw back before they begin to learn. From a distance, tenth-century Medieval Latin textbooks for school children may sound pretty dull, but such a textbook can reveal attitudes toward religion that would surprise almost any inhabitant of the twentieth century. With some reading, some research, some imagination to translate what is read into human experience, any topic can become absorbing. But until you get started you may not know that. It is better, then, to start with one of your present interests.

What if I Don't Have Any Interests?

If you feel that you haven't any interests, you are probably thinking that you have no "academic" interests or that you have no "hobby," like collecting stamps or butterflies. Many students are so busy working or helping their families after school that they haven't had the extra time to follow their personal interests very far. But they may feel inadequate if a teacher asks about "interests." This natural feeling is actually the result of defining "interests" too narrowly. Moreover, one major purpose of education and study is to find and develop interests—formerly called "talents," and now termed, somewhat pompously, "potentialities." At this stage you may not know what your own interests are, or you may think secretly that you have no intellectual interests, a possible but unlikely state. Probably, without your noticing it, your interest temperature goes up and down a thousand times a day. Part of the problem of the question "What should I write about?" is "What interests me?" Again, writing leads back to introspection and onward to developing awareness of one's own mind.

How Can I Learn About My Own Interests?

It may be important for you to start taking your intellectual pulse more often. If you pay more attention to your own thoughts during the day, and ask yourself what you are thinking about more often, you will discover that you have many interests. These can be pursued, deepened, and made more informed if you will recognize them and begin to nurture them more consciously. Further, since great literature draws upon the deepest sources of human nature, you can find all of your more serious and most of your trivial interests in it, but this can be said of most art forms.

How Can I Relate My Interests to Writing Topics?

Suppose all you know is that you are interested in people? Why not follow that interest? What is the population of your city block or your hometown? Have your neighbors lived there for many years, or are some of them new to the area? What caused people to move to your area? What local businesses employ most of the people who live near you? How do most people get to work? Are there some people whose lives and opinions seem to you quite remarkable for some reasons that are not associated with what we call "success?" Collect a few questions about local or national issues that seem to concern your own family, and ask them of your neighbors. You will be surprised at the results. All towns and segments of large cities have their individual problems: the local industry laying off workers, the planning of the new highway, the closing down of old apartment houses, the arrival of a large discount center. Most people are surprised to discover the issues that concern their neighbors, and often the variety of attitudes toward these issues is greater than you might expect. At everyone's hand there are literally thousands of subjects related to that expressed "interest in people."

But how can that "interest in people" be used in the more traditional classes that are devoted to reading of short stories, plays, and novels? Again, follow your interest. What kind of a defense can be fashioned for the villain of the story or for some historical personage who has a bad name? Take the piece of literature being studied and try to deduce the character of the narrator. Criticize the hero. Don't suppose that an interest in basketball, or harpooning, or medicine, or movies has nothing to do with writing. "Oh well, that's a personal interest, but this is history (or English)." That is an old-fashioned attitude. From one point of view, history is nothing but life stories, and literature is gossip at a grand level. Take, for example, even *Hamlet,* one of Shakespeare's greatest tragedies, and take a student interested almost exclusively in sports. If the student reads the play carefully, there is something in it for him. A paper might focus on Hamlet, the athlete. He is portrayed, primarily, as an intellectual, but how bookish and inactive is he? He does stab Polonius in speedy reaction. He had been practicing fencing before his last duel with Laertes. He did leap onto the pirate ship before anyone else. Could an examination of Hamlet's energetic nature lead to a better understanding of this so-called inactive procrastinator. Almost any idea that interests you can provide a starting place for an essay or for a research paper.

How Should I Begin Preparation for the Paper?

Prewriting time is spent moving from the general to the particular, from a consideration of the general topic and its various parts to a selection of the particular angle that you will use for your essay. It is wise not to try to decide on your paper's subject until you have gained perspective on the general topic. For this larger view why not begin by reading an article in the *Encyclopaedia Britannica* before you consider further? Somewhere within this larger presentation is the smaller topic you will choose to be the subject of your paper.

For the nonresearch as well as for the research essay, it is useful to jot down all the basic questions you can think of about the general topic assigned. Suppose you were given a series of general subjects and you chose "television." The topic is too general; how can it be made suitable for an essay? If you list related questions, possibilities for research and for a focus are likely to emerge.

- Why is television important?
- How does it influence people?

- Is the extent of its present influence known?
- What is the evidence that it shapes attitudes?
- From another approach, how is the experience of viewing television different from that of reading?
- How is it different from attending the theater?
- Does television experience train actors differently than does stage experience?
- What are the advantages and disadvantages in television financed by means other than advertising?
- How might television be made more beneficial than it is?
- How would "beneficial" be defined?
- What are the dangers in controlling television?

As you begin to note questions, many new aspects of any subject appear. "What should I write?" becomes "What is there to write about?" That question then becomes "Which will I choose?"

Which Topic, or Group of Related Topics, Shall I Choose to Give My Paper Unity?

The general topic of television is too big for thorough coverage in a few pages. You could write on "The Importance of Television" or "The Advantages of Cable Television." You might prefer to study "Problems of Producing a Serial on TV." You will find that general subjects must be limited if they are to be treated thoroughly and if your research is to be efficient. If you spend one week reading about the history of television, that week may be well spent for your own general information, but the information probably will not be directly pertinent to your writing if your topic is "Serial Production" or "Acting on TV." The earlier you can decide on a limited topic for your paper, the more efficient your research time can be.

After I Have Chosen My Topic for Research and Have Read up on It, How Do I Focus the Paper?

The focus, the angle—or expressed more formally, the thesis—is crucial to all essays, research or nonresearch, academic or journalistic. No matter how many critics the writer reads, or how many sources, the paper is, in the end, his own. All information, all quoted authorities selected, every choice regarding sequence of paragraphs must be made in relation to the writer's dominating thesis. The introduction asserts the thesis; the paper demonstrates it, expands upon it, illustrates it, defines it, contrasts it with other views. The thesis is both the heart of the paper's content and the major determinant of its organization.

What Is the Thesis?

The thesis probably is stated in a declarative sentence drawn from one of the major questions first jotted down. If you select the topic "The Importance of Television," the thesis statement might be "Television's importance has been greatly overrated." For the paper topic "How does television influence people?" your thesis statement might be "Television is essentially a nationwide supermarket designed to sell goods, not drama, or humor, or education. The television shows are sold to television not because they are intelligent or sound, but because they can guarantee the widest possible market of viewers. Therefore, the blandest, least independent minded and most universally appealing opinions will always be presented on television."

The thesis usually is an opinion. An essay, even a single paragraph, needs an opinion to get it going, some idea that can be developed, argued, supported. (For convenience and clarity, the term "thesis statement" is being used to refer to the paper's central idea, and "topic sentence" is used to refer to the expression of a paragraph's central idea.) Unspecific as it is, "I like television" is a better thesis statement than "My family just bought a television set." The first statement can be developed more easily than an event-statement can. "X million Americans bought television sets last year" is not a thesis statement, although it could be used to support the thesis that television is potentially a powerful advertising medium.

It is true that a controversial thesis statement is more apt to engage curiosity than a conventional one. "Really intelligent people enjoy only the stupid shows on television" would probably engage your reader's interest, at least until he found out how you resolved the riddle. However, looking for the controversial thesis to find a fresh edge for the topic can often lead to an arrogant quality that will put your reader off and end by counter-persuading him. These decisions require tact and depend upon your perception of your audience. You know that everyone agrees that television should be improved, so you would avoid offering that idea as your thesis statement. You must cast about until you find an idea that you believe in firmly enough to be able to support it thoroughly, an idea that is an interesting angle on an old subject. And do not be apologetic about your subject's being old. All subjects are old and have been so since before Ecclesiastes said that there was nothing new under the sun. The only things that are new are insights, new combinations, fresh perspectives on the old—like new discoveries of old principles, old facts examined through a recent theory, an old play considered from a different viewpoint, ancient emotions in a new context. The world of experience is always new to each individual, but he must be aware that he is the new thing in the old context. His responses are precious to him and to others, if he can express them. Still, they must be said freshly, or their subjective newness will not come through. ''Love is blind'' may be a new and painful insight to you, gained recently, but unless some way beyond that particular cliché is found to express it, the truth of it will not be communicated to others.

Consider this group of sentences. Which ones would you choose as best for expansion in a paragraph or in an essay?

- My family bought a car last week.
- The automobile has changed America.

Those two sentences are very different. The second is clearly more helpful.

- My family never has any luck with cars.
- The day my father gave up driving was a happy day for all of us.

Funny essays might be developed from either of these.

- Many people are contemptuous of bird watchers.
- The warblers nesting in our rhododendrons changed our family's routine.

125

Try to give useful thesis statements for these general subjects: "sports," "college," "cars," "friends," "newspapers," "commuting," "population," "elections." A useful thesis statement would be a clear assertion, perhaps controversial, that is "developable."

research

What Is the Difference Between the Research and the Nonresearch Essay?

Most writing, even short-story writing, requires some research. The "familiar" essay that appears to be fairly casual and informal, rather in the manner of John Fischer's regular column in *Harper's* called "The Easy Chair," actually requires solid research. The earliest familiar essays, like those of Michel de Montaigne in the sixteenth century, gently ruminative as they are, move in wide-ranging fashion among many books, ancient and contemporary, and with much observation of the natural world, although they do not have the air of having been researched. The term "familiar essay" refers to the tone of the essay, written apparently for a circle of familiars or friends. The more formal essay, or "exposition," uses a firmly structured pattern and tends to follow the model of Matthew Arnold and Thomas Babington Macaulay in that they are "public," not "familiar," essays.

They often aim to persuade the unknown readers of the writer's opinion. The author of the familiar essay, however, aims more often merely to think aloud, to present personal observations in thoughtful fashion.

The familiar essayist may discuss, as Montaigne does, his attitudes toward books, the kind he likes, those he thinks are trivial. He may draw in a comment on his cat or on his own inability to read "by attack" and force himself to read a book he finds difficult. (He puts it aside to try again later.) The more formal essayist, writing for "the public," may exclude "I" entirely. By his formality he may give the impression, as Matthew Arnold does, that he is an institution, like a school or a library. That is, of course, an extreme, but quite common in some scholarly journals.

Today in journalism the two genres—the public, or formal, essay and the familiar essay—are mixed. Editorials present the editor's personal view in formal manner or in extreme and personal fashion. Film critics, like Renata Adler and Rex Reed, write sharply perceptive personal evaluations for a public audience and do not assume the ease and familiarity with their wide audiences that John Fischer's essays do. Yet Fischer's essays often attempt to persuade the audience of an opinion or a course of action, and, by so doing, his familiar essays adopt the purpose of the more formal essay of persuasion. In addition, the New Journalism tends to emphasize the writer as witness to his times and no longer attempts to achieve objective reporting as did journalism of ten to fifteen years ago. Many New Journalists think that the objective manner of the formal writers led the audience to think it received The Truth and not the author's view. The objective manner, they think, obscured the author's bias. For these reasons, principally, New Journalists now admit to their personal angles and present them vividly. Their assumption seems to be that a reader must read many articles in order to surround the truth and come to his personal estimation of what is going on in the world.

Many schools require a grasp of the formal exposition for use in writing research papers for almost every class—English, sociology, French, Spanish, history, political science, or psychology. For this reason the more formal exposition or research paper will be treated now. Often, English writing classes begin with autobiographical essays that follow the model of the familiar essay in its personal tone and content, or they may develop a New Journalism in their classes. For these writing classes the discussions of the structure of the research essay that follow will be pertinent, but the note-taking techniques, for example, may not apply to the writing of interviews. Some teachers approve a manner that is more personal than the one this book endorses for the research paper. These matters depend on many variables, including taste and personality. My personal view is that the formal exposition that presents research findings directly and the conclusions drawn from them should not presume familiarity with its reader and should not use "I," because the so-called objective truth being presented must exist apart from the subjective viewer. It does not depend upon the writer's individuality for its truth. The familiar essay—which is often autobiographical in content, and which depends on the lore of the individual essayist, his acute personal insights, and his subjective impressions—should make no effort to suppress the "I." The "I" is intrinsic to the material being presented.

However you may come to view these matters, the research paper is as personal a piece of work in one sense as the familiar essay. It is the author's presentation of fact and opinion that is derived from primary and secondary sources and from his own thinking about these. The organization, selection, and slanting of the material are all his. He may not express his opinions directly, but just as the New Journalists said of the Old Guard, he expresses his views indirectly through his techniques of organization and selection. Many students think that the research paper is not their own, but is, rather, the ideas of other people passed along to the reader with quotations and footnotes. If a research paper is such a cut-and-paste collection of sources, it is undiscriminating and lacks the author's proper control. The research paper requires all the imagination and creativity that the familiar essay requires, even though its presentation may be more formal and less personal. Both the familiar essay and the more formal research paper may use research, and both must distinguish between fact and opinion. The searching out and use of primary and secondary sources are problems more central to the research paper than to the familiar essay, but both must present arguments logically and effectively with appropriate illustrations. Both employ the same techniques of paragraph development, and both depend upon precision of language. In short, problems faced and skills gained in coping with one kind of essay can be transferred to writing the other, just as scholarly writing can use the vividness and grace of the journalist, and the press can use the scholar's respect for accuracy.

When Is a Fact an Opinion?

Most people are pretty clear about the obvious differences between fact and opinion. They know that "It is raining," said with the hand catching rain drops, is a statement of fact and "I think it is raining," said by someone walking to the window, is a statement of conjecture. "Plenty of rain is what these roses need" is opinion. It may be correct or not, depending on how much rain the plants received in the last week, but when it was said, it was opinion. An opinion can be expressed firmly as if it were fact, and a factual statement may be incorrect. Begin to be attentive to fact, opinion, and the opinion that sounds like fact. Are the following statements fact or opinion?

- Wearing rubber boots in the house is bad for one's circulation.
- Melville published *Moby Dick* when he was thirty-two.
- Swimming is the most relaxing of sports.
- The Narragansett Indians once occupied Rhode Island.
- Polo was first developed in India.
- Glasses worn too early are bad for one's eyes.
- Vergil asked for the *Aeneid* to be burned at his death.
- Mark Twain's skepticism shows in his short stories.

Of these statements, which sound like facts and would need to be checked? Which sound like superstition? Which sound like opinion or an interpretation of personal experience and judgment? Some fascinating research can be done in the effort to distinguish between fact and pseudofact.

What Is the Difference Between Primary and Secondary Sources?

Critical materials, that is, pieces of writing about plays, novels, poetry, are called secondary sources. The primary sources of literary criticism are the plays, novels, poetry themselves. Reviews or critical discussions of literature or films are secondary sources. A history book is a secondary source in the sense that it draws its data from primary sources and other secondary sources. Its primary sources are treaties, wills, diaries, letters, or newspapers and other writings of the time. But, if a later student investigates the writing of history and wants to know how historians of the time viewed events, the writings of the older historian may become a primary source. Today's journalists are, in their own time, secondary sources, because they draw their material from interviews, newspapers, books, but to a later historian they will be "writings of the time," or primary sources.

The good research paper offers a balance of primary and secondary sources. This balance is vital, because the opinions of critics must be checked against the facts as they are known. Every generation rewrites history, not in George Orwell's sense by deliberately erasing or willfully masking what happened in the past, but usually because it discovers that the views of past historians were dominated by some selective bias. Historians have written with religious or sectarian biases and have supported Anglicans, Presbyterians, Christians, Jews, and Muslims. They have had political biases and supported Yorkists, Lancastrians, Whigs or Tories, Republicans or Democrats. Intentionally and unintentionally they have had racial, sex, and class biases. Their biases may influence the way they report events, but often the biases are not immediately clear. The reader must examine the reports of several events and compare them with those of other historians to begin to grasp a historian's bias. This is not to say that no historian should be believed, but that every reader should be skeptical of what he reads. If the researcher can get behind the history text to the primary sources of the times—their stories, diaries, letters, paintings—he will have a more exciting time doing his research. In that way, even if in a small way, he will be a historian himself, and then he must watch his own biases.

How Do I Go About Research?

That question, broad as it is, is the sensible one most students want to ask and are afraid to ask, because they suppose everyone knows but themselves. Because they don't ask, teachers suppose they know, give them a topic, and send them to the library. The students often avoid the library, go to a bookstore and ask for "a book on the history of music," or they buy *Monarch's* or *Cliff's Notes* on the book or play being studied. The whole procedure is quite short-sighted, because the capsule education they buy may turn them away from the real thing.

Instead, draw up as many questions as you can on the general topic, as you do for the nonresearch paper.

- What is the subject?
- How is it defined?
- What parts of it can you see, even at this point in research?
- Why is the topic important?
- Has it been much discussed?
- Are there radically different views of the subject?

First, get the large perspective, the "overview," of the subject, realizing that it must be narrowed down to a small segment of the larger topic.

How Large Should the Small Segment Be?

This cannot be known specifically so early in research planning, but essentially you should work to make the subject narrow enough to be treated thoroughly within whatever number of pages the teacher permits. Very little can be treated fully in five pages. Narrow the subject down, for example, from warfare in the Middle Ages to the arrival of the stirrup in western Europe in the first part of the eighth century.

To find the answers to his questions, the student will need to read, but what should he read? Now, his bibliography becomes vital. He may go obediently to the library, but what will he look for there? The card catalogue? In the card catalogue he will find only those books that have his subject in their titles. How many will have "stirrup" in their titles? And, of course, he knows that many subjects are treated in books that are not mentioned in their titles. The student needs some bibliographical guides.

What Is Bibliography?

Broadly speaking, bibliography is the study of all aspects of the book. It refers, in this general sense, to bookmaking, paper, print, early editions, illuminations, bindings. Bibliographers are the super sleuths of literary criticism, using the latest scientific techniques— including analysis under infrared light, dating editions by watermarks on their paper, and studying the ingredients of the ink— they can often provide factual data that help the literary critic understand his subject.

But the term "bibliography" also refers to lists of books and articles on selected topics, like glass-blowing, censorship, or Milton. Most students are surprised to learn about the tremendous amount of bibliographical help available to them. When a student first begins to work on research, he should consult the *Bibliographic Index: A Cumulative Bibliography of Bibliographies, 1937–date* (New York: H. W. Wilson, 1945–date) to discover if a bibliography already exists on his subject. A published bibliography would shorten research time, because the writer would need only to add to it titles written after its date of publication.

Each field—literature, the social sciences, religion, education, fine and performing arts, science and technology—has its own bibliographies, although some listings are more generally useful than others and may be used across fields. A booklet like *The Research Paper: Gathering Library Material, Organizing and Preparing the Manuscript,* by Lucyle Hook and Mary Virginia Gaver (Englewood Cliffs, N.J.: Prentice-Hall, 1969), would be exceedingly helpful to use as a guide. This particular text describes each bibliographical guide it mentions, explaining to the student how it might be used.

In actuality, every student needs to make his own list of titles to read or scan for his paper. Faced with acres of titles from 1890 to the present, what should you do? You should not begin to read indiscriminately. One way to gain some guidance is to select and read the most recent review article on your subject. Its title might be "A Review of the Controversy Concerning the Pentagon Papers" or "Control of the Press in the U.S., 1960–1970." Usually a good review article will refer to recent articles, and from its footnotes you can cull a useful starting bibliography. In addition, it will provide an idea about attitudes of authors. If an approach is uncongenial to you, you can be warned off early. Not all titles are equally reliable, of course. Consult the bibliographies listed in histories of literature, textbooks, recent encyclopedia articles, biographies considered authoritative, and recent editions. Authors of works of that kind list in their bibliographies books and articles that they consider significant.

How Do I Find a Bibliography on My Subject?

After checking with the *Bibliographic Index,* just mentioned, see the *Subject Guide to Books in Print.* The *Subject Guide to Books in Print: An Index to the Publisher's Trade List Annual. 1956–date* (New York: R. R. Bowker, 1956–date), will tell you which books now in print—that is, available for purchase in the United States—treat your subject. The following publications list books in English in print from 1928 according to author, title, and subject: the *United States Catalog; Books in Print January 1, 1928* (New York: H. W. Wilson, 1928), and the *Cumulative Book Index: A World List of Books in the English Language, 1928–date* (New York: H. W. Wilson, 1933–date).

Then consult the *Reader's Guide.* The *Reader's Guide to Periodical Literature, 1900–date* (New York: H. W. Wilson, 1905–date), is one of the most useful magazine indexes. It indexes magazine articles every month, and issues a compilation of monthly editions every three months. For research on current issues, biography, scientific investigations, literary and historical topics, the *Reader's Guide* is invaluable. Items are listed under subject and title.

Helpful earlier works include: *Nineteenth Century Reader's Guide to Periodical Literature, 1890–1899, with Supplementary Indexing, 1900–1922* (New York: H. W. Wilson, 1944), and *Poole's Index to Periodical Literature, 1802–81* (Boston: Houghton Mifflin, 1891). These publications permit you to investigate treatments of your subject in periodical literature back to 1902, but *Poole's Index* lists by subject not author.

How Should I Collect My Bibliography?

Gather your bibliography on small cards, putting one title on each card. List the author's last name first so you can alphabetize your bibliography cards later, and underline titles of books and magazines. Put quotation marks around the title of articles, short stories, and poems.

> Donohue, Agnes McNeil, ed.
> A Casebook on The Grapes of Wrath
> New York : Thomas y. Crowell, 1968

Your collection of cards will constitute your own reading bibliography, that list from which you will select reading that will form the research for your paper. Keep it flexible by writing the title of only one book or article on each card. Often a brief comment jotted on the back of the card after you have read the article can be useful later.

Must All Papers Include Bibliographies?

Students are often asked to prepare and present bibliographies before they begin research so the teacher may be assured that the students know about some of the most useful books or sources for reference. To do research, you need your own working bibliography, but not all papers must include a last page or pages that list the books used in the paper. Most articles, including those published in scholarly journals do not, as a rule, include bibliographies. The footnotes of the article contain the texts cited in the article, with full bibliographical information, although in footnote form. You must ask your teacher whether or not he requires a bibliography to be included at the end of your research paper.

What Is the Correct Form of the Bibliography Presented at the End of a Finished Paper?

The bibliography presented at the end of the finished paper will be alphabetized according to the author's last name. It will be entitled, according to the writer's decision and the teacher's advice, something like, "A Selected Bibliography" or "List of Works Consulted." Rarely would you present in your paper a complete bibliography of all the works you had found written on your subject. Usually you would list the books and articles consulted for your paper or those cited in it. Many schools and colleges have style manuals that they recommend for model footnote and bibliographical form. Yet, in the same school or college history and English departments may follow different style manuals. For the correct form of the bibliographical listing in any paper, discover the form manual suggested by the department for which the paper is being prepared, and use it carefully, with attention to its conventions of capitalizing, underlining, parentheses, and so forth.

If your school or department has not chosen a style manual or stated a preference for bibliographical form, you can use the pattern given below which follows the Modern Language Association's *M L A Style Sheet,* (2nd ed., 1970). Imagine that what follows is part of the bibliography of a paper on Steinbeck's *The Grapes of Wrath.*

LIST OF WORKS CONSULTED

Beach, Joseph Warren. *American Fiction, 1920–1940.* New York: Macmillan, 1942.

Carpenter, Frederic I. "The Philosophical Joads." *College English,* 2 (January 1941), 312–25.

Donohue, Agnes McNeil, ed. A Casebook on the Grapes of Wrath. New York: Thomas Y. Crowell, 1968.

Hunter, J. P. "Steinbeck's Wine of Affirmation in the *Grapes of Wrath." Essays in Modern American Literature.* Ed. Richard E. Langford. Deland, Florida: Stetson Univ. Press, 1963, pp. 76–89.

Shockley, Martin. "The Reception of the *Grapes of Wrath* in Oklahoma." *American Literature,* 15 (Jaunary 1944), 351–61.

The first item exemplifies the form used for a book by one author. The second and fifth show the form used for articles that appeared in journals, *American Literature* and *College English.* The third item gives the correct form for a collection of essays compiled by an editor. The fourth item is an example of the form used to cite an article taken from a collection of essays.

Am I Supposed to Read All the Books and Articles That I Find at the Beginning of My Research?

In the best of all possible worlds, you might be expected to make a complete listing of all the books and articles written about your subject, to read them all, and then to write a brilliantly informed analysis. Granted limited time and energy, you have to plan quite arbitrarily: so much time for research, and for writing, revision, and footnote checking. Your general procedure should be to list general questions about your topic, gain an overview of the subject, add further questions, gather bibliography that will include both primary and secondary sources and both standard and more recent secondary material, and read from that bibliography until the specific topic of your paper is chosen and until you feel fairly secure about your thesis and your illustrations in support of it.

How Can I Know When I Have Read Enough to Write the Paper?

There is always more to be known. If you waited until you had no more questions on a subject before writing, you would not live long enough to write a paragraph. This is true of all writers. Research has to stop before all the questions are answered. Still, about a narrow subject, information and interpretation can be sound. Try to read to the limits of the recent material, until the attitudes and interpretations begin to repeat and the experts begin to refer to material that you have already studied.

With Everything That Has Been Written,
What Have I to Say?

First, shifts in times and attitudes permit new insights. Second, much of the information that appears to be confirmed is conjecture. In some ways, history is a tissue of facts, suppositions, conjecture, clues, and interpretation. There is no conspiracy concealing this fact. Rather, most writers have, sensibly, concentrated on what is known or accepted. Still, the result of not saying what is unknown is that many students feel depressed, as if they had been born after everything had been said. The reverse is true. Even birth and death dates of major writers are still unverified; Chaucer's dates, for instance, are accepted by a kind of gentlemanly consensus, but they have not been proved, and probably cannot be proved. And behind the known facts there are usually clusters of unknown material that have been passed over. Many people know that Sir Thomas Malory was the author of that greatest collection of stories about Arthur and his knights, the *Morte Arthur,* but, in fact, we do not know which Sir Thomas Malory. Five centuries after his death, and in the last ten years, a new book has appeared with a new candidate for the identity of the Sir Thomas Malory.

The daily newspaper indicates that contemporary events are also an intriguing web of fact and speculation, of clues and interpretations. Did the President say this or that? Did his words have this particular meaning or that one? What might this new "clarification" of his words mean to the country's economy? And so forth. Because all events are so complex, and because new evidence about past events does keep emerging, there will always be more to say.

How Can I Keep My Own Ideas if I Have
to Read the Professionals?

The central subject is the text (or primary source or event) and its meaning. Every possible approach to understanding is worthy of respect, but the aim is understanding of the subject. Anyone can be intimidated by the polished, trained professional who writes confidently, drawing upon volumes of illustrative material. At first, anyone is convinced that every writer he reads is right. The cure for this is not, however, to avoid reading the critics, but to cope with them. Your independence of mind will be nurtured if you always go back to your primary source (literary text, treaty, lawyer's statement, state-ment of the diarist, or whatever) and test the critic's statement against the primary source. If you hold in your mind that you aim to under-stand "the truth," however complex that may be, then you will find yourself less intimidated by the professional. If he is right, he should be followed; if he is not, you should know why you think he is wrong.

If I Like What I Think, Why Should I Read the Professionals?

The only reason to read the critics or any professional's writing on any subject is to get beyond one's own mind and its limitations. If you like what you think and do not want to be intruded upon by opposing views, there is no reason to read. Presumably, however, the author had an "intention," some effect he was working to achieve and to communicate. Presumably, the reader would like to understand what the author aimed to achieve. The professional literary historian, for example, can often inform the layman about earlier meanings of words, the conventions of writing, the conditions of living at the time that can bring the student closer to understanding the author's probable meaning. But even the professional cannot know an author's "intention." It remains to be deduced from his works, usually without a great deal of external evidence (that is, evidence from outside the work itself, such as letters or diaries) that might apply to the work and suggest the conditions of writing.

Some people say that the work of art is what it is in the time the spectator looks at it or reads it or hears it, that it changes over the centuries in relation to what the audience sees in it. Others feel that one should try by every means to see what the author wrote in his own time and, in addition, try to distinguish what later times might emphasize or "see" in the work. Letters, biographies, maps, dictionaries, stage directions, wills, treaties, critical interpretations—all can help you to understand the meaning of the work when it was written. They help you to move beyond the limitations of your own mind (time, nationality, locale, language, customs, attitudes, informa-tion) and to understand a product of another time and locale. For example, a dictionary composed on historical principles will tell you that "silly" in the fourteenth century meant many things: happy, blissful, spiritually blessed, innocent, good, poor, and wretched. If you read an early poem giving the word "silly" its twentieth-century meaning, you would be imposing on the poem a meaning that the author did not write.

There is no law against preferring to read a work and experience its effect without the intrusion of other voices, but if you make that choice, you must be aware that the poem or novel you are reading and experiencing may not be the one the author wrote, but the one you are imagining. The difficulties in reading Camus' popular novel *The Stranger* provide an interesting example of this.

Many people see the hero of *The Stranger* as numb, listless, and indifferent to everything, including his sweetheart and his mother. Camus wrote a preface to his novel in 1955 because, according to Philip Thody, certain critics had said the hero, Meursault, was "a schizophrenic" or "a moron," that he was "an example of the mechanization and depersonalization of modern life."[1] Camus' preface asserts, however, that Meursault was utterly honest; that he "is condemned because he does not play the game." Camus explains his title:

> In this respect, he is foreign to the society in which he lives; he wanders, on the fringe, in the suburbs of private, solitary, sensual life. And this is why some readers have been tempted to look upon him as a piece of social wreckage. A much more accurate idea of the character, or, at least, one much closer to the author's intentions, will emerge if one asks just *how* Meursault doesn't play the game. The reply is a simple one: he refuses to lie. To lie is not only to say what isn't true. It is also and above all, to say *more* than is true, and, as far as the human heart is concerned, to express more than one feels. This is what we all do, every day, to simplify life. He says what he is, he refuses to hide his feelings, and immediately society feels threatened.[2]

Perhaps those who read the work without reading Camus' 1955 preface to the American edition or those who thought it was the story of a schizophrenic or of what modern life can do to a man, enjoyed the book. But what they enjoyed was not, apparently, what Camus wrote, but what they saw in what he wrote. They can elect to prefer what they first saw after they know what the author meant to write, but they should be aware that they are choosing to read their own thoughts, not his.

note taking

Is There a Good Way to Take Notes for the Research Paper?

The note-taking method should suit the problems of research and the product desired. Unquestionably, some ways of taking notes inhibit flexibility and some encourage it. Although note taking on long sheets of paper may be suitable for research based on interviews, for example, for other kinds of research—for a study, perhaps, that includes the views of various literary critics—notes taken on long pages can cause difficulties. For one thing, in rereading the notes, you will be encouraged to think in terms of critics and what each said, not in terms of the ideas debated. Although the notes are arranged by critics (on long sheets of paper), your writing will have to be organized by ideas. Thus, your ability to relate ideas, to see disagreement among critics will be inhibited. In that instance, the note-taking method works against your paper's needs.

A worse result can occur if you should write on both sides of those long sheets. When you come to writing your paper, you will take to scissors, to writing arrows and drawing stars, and to using different colors of pencil—all to make clear to yourself which spokesman is which and whom you should quote first and second. The air can seem to be full of fluttering pages as panic rises and order has to be brought out of confusion. Good people take to retyping their notes; lesser minds reread books four or five times to find that lost quotation; some give up and go to the movies. No wonder scholarship loses lively minds to space travel.

Remember that your notes will be used later to organize your paper and finally to provide footnotes. To help the later stages of your work, try to follow a consistent method at the early stage. If you take notes on small four-by-six inch note slips, and if you make sure to write one item (one idea, one fact, one image, one concept with its support) per note slip, then the later tasks of organization and footnote preparation will be greatly eased. This method seems laborious to people until they try it; then they see that it simplifies both note taking and note organizing remarkably.

How Does One Item per Note Slip Help Organization of the Research Paper?

One article covers many subjects, even though all subjects may serve to support the writer's thesis. As you study one article, you may take notes on many subjects. If these notes are separated, jotted down with one item per note slip, they can be interrelated with other articles later. By this method you would put a brief title (a word or a phrase) at the top of the card to indicate the subject of that card. "Early schooling" or "Sun imagery" or "Dangers of marijuana" would be enough to help you later in sorting your notes. In a research paper on drugs, for example, many experts will take various positions, agreeing on some dangers of marijuana and disagreeing on others. If all notes are kept with one item per note slip, you can reread your notes and gather all discussions of one danger of marijuana together as well as all the arguments that deny that danger. The primary gain of the one-item-per-note-slip method is flexibility.

A second gain is the ability to visualize the major segments of research. After two or three weeks of reading on one topic, you will find probably that all the writers or parties to a dispute have been discussing just a few major problems. The notes reveal this division by falling automatically into separate topics. You can sort these separate issues into different stacks of note slips and then consider them. You can decide which segment leads on most easily to the next, which is a good lead-off idea, and which is the major idea that deserves the most important (the last) position in the paper. You can begin to plan transitions from one major section of your paper to the next. At this time it becomes clear why it is so useful to have made notes on your own thoughts and opinions; they can be filed right along with those of the other critics.

What Kind of Notes Should I Take?

In general, paraphrase the useful idea or fact; that is, put it into your own words. Quote only what is both vital to your argument and well said. You can paraphrase most useful material and relate it more firmly to your own paper by the rewording than by direct quotation. But a controversial statement that you plan to dispute should be retained and quoted precisely. For your proper "victory," it must be clear that the opponent was defeated on the argument he offered and not by a twisting of his meaning.

How Many Notes Should I Take?

It is hard, perhaps impossible, to strike the perfect balance about note taking before the paper's focus has been decided. Some people favor a highly selective note-taking method, but that can require later rereading to find facts that were overlooked in the first reading. There is much to say in support of unselective note taking before the paper's specific subject is chosen. If at the beginning of research you note whatever seems striking, interesting, significant, and possibly relevant, you permit yourself a wide range of possible topics. Often, following this method, the matter that seemed urgent at first begins to seem less interesting, as some other idea or problem begins to emerge as more challenging. Something that seemed to be minor at the beginning of research often turns out to be vital, or your interest may shift as your information grows.

Extensive note taking permits growth and flexibility, but it does use more time and energy than does highly selective note taking. If time does not allow you this vagrant curiosity, a high degree of selectivity should be settled on from the start, and you should read just to answer those early questions listed. In any case, as soon as the specific topic for the paper is chosen, note taking must become highly selective.

What Form Should I Use for My Note Slips?

Try to establish a method to follow consistently. One workable scheme is this: the first time you use any book or article, write on a note slip the book or article's complete bibliographical reference: its author, title, place and date of publication, editors, volume, page numbers—whatever information will be needed later. It is also wise to add the library call number to save time in case you should wish to refer to that text again. From then on as you take notes, put on the left side of each note slip the author's last name only, a shortened form of the book title (underlined) or the article (surrounded by quotation marks), and the page from which the material was taken. In the center and at the top of the card, write a shortened title for the slip that indicates its contents:

Character of Meursault - truthlover

Thody, ed.
Lyrical Essays
p. 336

In 1955 preface to the American edition of _The Stranger_, Camus denied M. was a victim of society's mechanization. Camus said: " he is animated by... a passion for the absolute and for truth."

How Should I Take Notes on a Quotation?

If the author's words are used, put quotation marks around his exact words, use spaced periods to indicate ellipses (any words omitted)—three spaced periods to indicate an omission within a sentence, and four (three for the ellipsis and one for the sentence period) to indicate omission after a completed sentence. A note on the Camus preface might look this way:

> Camus' preface: Meursault truthlover
>
> Thody, ed.
> Lyrical Essays
> p. 336
>
> "A much more accurate idea of the character... will emerge if one asks just _how_ Meursault doesn't play the game. The reply is a simple one: he refuses to lie... He says what he is, he refuses to hide his feelings; and immediately society feels threatened."

The first ellipsis indicates omission of material within a sentence. The second indicates an omission of material after a completed sentence. There is no need for signs of ellipsis after "threatened," even though the source continues for many sentences, because "threatened" ends the sentence and the note does not quote further.

How Do I Paraphrase in a Note?

The paraphrase attempts to say what the author said but in words other than his. This note uses a short remark of Camus' and a paraphrase:

Camus says in his preface to the
1955 American edition of The
Stranger that Meursault "refuses
to lie." He says that Meursault
won't tell untruths but he won't
exaggerate either —

Thody, ed.
Lyrical Essays
p.336

The author's emphasis, however, as well as his content should be
clear in the paraphrase. Paraphrasing takes care and tact, a genuine
wish to express the author's meaning. It is easy to betray an author's
meaning in a paraphrase, to disagree with him as you write the note
and put his emphasis wrong so that you express your own emphasis,
not his. Then when you want to use that note, it will mislead you.

Can Notes Be a Combination of Quotations and Paraphrasing?

That combination can be very useful. The quotation can catch
the author's emphasis precisely in the tricky material, and the paraphrase can generalize for the simpler ideas. The paper rests upon
the quality of the notes. An exact quotation may be exceedingly
useful for your later understanding, even if you decide not to quote
it in your paper. Your own note has to be precise in order to prevent
confusion later between the end of the author's words and the
beginning of your own paraphrase of his words. To illustrate, here
is a passage from a secondary source that you might use:

In 1348 a distinguished physician and astronomer, Giovanni
de' Dondi, began work with his own hands on a clock which it
took him sixteen years to complete. When it was finished in 1364,
Giovanni wrote a treatise describing it, equipped lavishly with

diagrams. Although six manuscripts of the work survive, this monument in the history of machinery has never been published. Giovanni's clock was only incidentally a timepiece: it included the celestial wanderings of sun, moon, and five planets, and provided a perpetual calendar of all religious feasts, both fixed and movable. His sense of the inter-relation of moving parts showed genius: to provide for the elliptical orbits of the Moon and Mercury (as required by the Ptolemaic system) he produced elliptical gears, and likewise made provision for the observed irregularities in the orbit of Venus. In complexity and refinement Giovanni's gearing goes enormously beyond anything which survives from earlier technology, including the fragments of the Hellenistic planetarium found in the Aegean Sea. In this aspect of machine design the fourteenth century marks an epoch. Indeed, no progress in the design of gravity-operated clocks seems to have been made during the next two centuries, for in 1529 when the Emperor Charles V visited Pavia and marvelled at Giovanni's clock, which was then out of order, he could find only one technician, Giovanni Torriani, capable of repairing it.[3]

Many kinds of notes might be written on this passage, depending on the researcher's purpose. Probably the only part of the passage that you might wish to quote would be the author's evaluation of Giovanni's achievement. The rest might be paraphrased in your notes. Your note slip containing the quotation might look this way:

14th cent machine design - Giovanni's clock

White
Medieval
Technology
p. 126

"In complexity + refinement Giovanni's gearing goes enormously beyond anything which survives from earlier technology, including the fragments of the Hellenistic planetarium found in the Aegean sea."

To be sure that you have the background you might need on the clock, you might make out one or two more note slips. One might say:

14ᵗʰ century machine design - Giovanni's clock

Giovanni de Dondi - clock, begun 1348 finished 1364, also recorded orbit of 5 planets and sun and moon, religious feast days, and time. Used "elliptical gears" for "elliptical orbits" of moon and Mercury according to Ptolemaic system.

White
Medieval
Technology
p. 126

Your own paper might use the two note slips in this way:

A clock, almost a mechanical calendar, finished by Giovanni de' Dondi in 1364, supplied evidence of Dondi's personal genius and of the advances in fourteenth-century design.[15] Lynn White claims, "In complexity and refinement Giovanni's gearing goes enormously beyond anything which survives from earlier technology, including the fragments of the Hellenistic planetarium found in the Aegean Sea."[16]

There, you give a footnote for both the facts of the first sentence and the quotation of the second. You quoted White because his statement was authoritative and emphatically stated, but you might have taken just the core of his remark, by saying:

Lynn White says that Giovanni de' Dondi's elliptical gearing shows an advance over "anything which survives from earlier technology,"[15] a powerful claim to make for a period that has been greatly underrated in respect to machine design.

But if your paper said the following, it would be plagiarism (illegal use of another person's words or ideas):

148

> Lynn White says that in refinement and complexity Giovanni's elliptical gearing surpassed anything that survives from earlier technology, including the parts of the Hellenistic planetarium discovered in the Aegean Sea.[15]

Even though you have reversed "complexity and refinement," used "surpassed" for "goes beyond anything," used "discovered" for "found" and "parts" for "fragments," and even though you have given a footnote, it is plagiarism. Change the sentence structure as well as the words to be sure that you have avoided using an author's words. Use a footnote for ideas and facts used that were unknown to you before you began research. Use quotation marks for words and phrases used in your source. A footnote number does not suffice to avoid plagiarism if the author's words or phrases appear in your paragraph. Many, many students miss this point and plagiarize quite innocently.

How Do Notes Become Footnotes?

At the end of research time, you will reread all of your notes slowly and sort them into separate subject piles. Later, when you begin to write, each of these small stacks will contain the data for one section of your paper, perhaps A of section II, for example. You will write up your notes (having remembered to include the notes on your own thoughts). Whenever you use a particular fact, interpretation, or quotation taken from one of the note slips (other than one on your own ideas), you will put a number, one space above the line, *after* the material taken from the critic. (Like this: [3]) You will write that same number on the note slip and put it aside. By the end of your writing, you may have any number of consecutively numbered notes; these are your footnotes.

Where Should Footnotes Be Written?

It is quite correct to type all footnotes, numbered in sequence and double spaced, at the end of the paper. It is no longer required to put footnotes at the bottom of each page and to number them separately for each page. All form manuals do not agree, however; you must follow the form preferred at your school.

What Should Be the Form of Footnotes and Bibliography?

The specific form for the paper depends upon the style manual adopted by the school or college. (The term "style manual" or "style sheet" does not refer to writing style, but to the preferred forms for punctuation in footnotes and bibliography.) Follow the style manual chosen by your school exactly, with attention to every comma, parenthesis, underlining, and space. Many students rebel against the rigidity of these conventions, but their aim is clarity, economy, accuracy, and usefulness, so that readers may share the gains of the writer's work. Further, there is this advantage: you need not invent a form for each reference. You can spend that time considering more interesting problems in the paper.

If your teacher has not recommended a form manual the following pattern, derived from the *M L A Style Sheet,* (2nd ed., 1970) may be used.

EXAMPLE FOOTNOTE PAGE

[1]Albert Camus, *The Stranger,* trans. Stuart Gilbert (New York: Alfred A. Knopf, 1946), p. 50. All quotations from *The Stranger* in my paper will use this edition. [A translated novel that will be cited throughout the paper.]

[2]Germaine Brée, *Camus* (New Brunswick: Rutgers Univ. Press, 1961), pp. 17–18. [A critical study by one author.]

[3]Jean Paul Sartre, "We Write for Our Own Time," *Virginia Quarterly Review,* 25, No. 1 (Spring 1947), rpt. in *A Casebook on Existentialism,* ed. William V. Spanos (New York: Thomas Y. Crowell, 1966), p. 151. [An article first printed in 1947 in the *Virginia Quarterly Review.* The footnote indicates that the author used the 1966 reprint.]

[4]Brée, Camus, p. 30. [Shows the shortened form appropriate for all second references.]

[5]Albert Camus, "An Absurd Reasoning," in *The Myth of Sisyphus and Other Essays,* trans. Justin O'Brien (New York: Alfred A. Knopf, 1955), p. 38. [Indicates that the author used an essay by Camus, entitled "An Absurd Reasoning," that was taken from his collection of essays *The Myth of Sisyphus and Other Essays.*]

[6]William V. Spanos, "Abraham, Sisyphus, and the Furies: Some Introductory Notes on Existentialism," in *Casebook,* ed. Spanos,

pp. 2–3. [The editor of the collection is treated just like another author of an essay in his collection, but the shortened form can be used because the collection has been cited; see footnote 3.]

[7]*Ibid.* pp. 9–11. [Uses the abbreviation for the Latin *ibidem,* "in the same place," to cite a second reference to the title immediately preceding.]

[8]Camus, *The Stranger,* p. 138. [Illustrates the shortened form permitted any reference after the first footnote reference.]

[9]Henri Peyre, "Camus the Pagan," *Yale French Studies,* No. 25 (Spring 1960), 23–25. [Demonstrates the correct form for an article (title within quotation marks) taken from a journal (underlined) from the 25th number (given in arabic numbers) printed in the spring of 1960.]

[10]Tom Towers, "The Truth, Again," *Herald Courier,* 25 October 1971, p. 7, cols. 2–3. [Using the name for the newspaperman satirized in Trollope's *The Warden,* this is an invented footnote to show the form for a piece from a daily newspaper.]

[11]Andrew S. Pringle-Pattison, "Philosophy," *Encyclopaedia Britannica,* 1911. [Illustrates correct form in citing a reference work that is arranged by alphabet. The article was signed with the initials "A. S. P.-P." A listing at the beginning of the volume identified the initials. If an encyclopedia article is unsigned, cite it by its title as it appears in the reference work.]

How Does a Paper Fit Together from All These Notes?

During research you may feel as if you are swimming in a vast lake, unable to see the shore in front or behind you. When you feel that way, refer to your initial questions, and go to the library determined to answer one of them that day—not all of them. After research, when you reread your notes, you will see that they fall into groups on separate topics. You may choose not to write on all the topics that your reading has covered. You should, in fact, try to avoid letting your paper be a restatement of your notes. It is wise, after reading your notes, to give yourself time to let the ideas gather in your mind.

Out of "all those notes," the ideas they trigger in your mind, and your own understanding of the primary sources must come some new patterning, some personal statement of interpretation or opinion. This personal formulation is the paper's central thesis. Each paragraph will be a presentation of some aspect of the thesis, or of some idea important to it. The paper moves, then, from a statement of the paper's subject, through demonstration of that thesis in the central paragraphs, called the body of the paper, to the conclusion or summary paragraph. In this sense the paper as a whole has the same structure that a paragraph does. Most paragraphs move from topic sentence, through illustration of the topic sentence, to concluding statement. As a writer, you are free, of course, to improvise. You can depart from this pattern in paragraphs of narrative description, dialogue, even fantasy, but essentially this basic structure supports the essay or research paper as a whole.

outlining

What Is the Point of Outlining?

Writing a long paper without outlining is like setting out in a car to go to Arkansas, thinking, "I'll look for signs; I think I go generally left." You may see California on the way, a pleasant experience, and you would find Arkansas probably, eventually, and perhaps without any disaster beyond fatigue. But such gallons of time and energy would be wasted that it would be better to concede in the first place and to pick up a free road map. The outline is the road map that you prepare before the trip. It need not be inflexible, and the plan might even be changed as you drive, but a long trip without a good map is unthinkable.

How Should I Prepare the Outline?

List the main points or topics that you wish to treat. Then arrange them in order of increasing importance, building from basic ideas to the most convincing or most significant. A working outline for a short paper might be a simple list of topics in logical sequence like this:

What is wrong with children's television
  (your list)
What television for children should be
  (your opinions)
Some suggestions for new programs for children
  (your ideas)

The longer research paper often works the other way (but not necessarily) and draws its outline mainly out of the notes. As you reread your notes, you will see that, because certain topics were discussed frequently in your reading, the notes "sort themselves" into those topics. Your own comments on the topics should be sorted in with those of the critics and the historians. As you relate these major topics to one another and plan which to present first in order to move logically to the second, third and fourth topics, you are planning your outline for the research paper.

What Is the Form of the Outline?

It is, essentially, a form to express logical relations. The conventions of lettering and indentation to be demonstrated merely express logical relations in a kind of visual aid. Consistency is important to show logic, but not merely for itself. The forms differ, and every student should inquire about the form favored at his own school, but here is a common one:

I. A main subject of the paper.
  A. A subordinate topic of main subject *I*.
  B. A subordinate topic related to *A*.
    1. A smaller subject, part of *B*, and therefore having some relation to *A*, but not a direct relationship.
    2. Another small subject associated with *1* and part of *B*.
II. A second major subject of the paper.
  A. A subordinate topic of main subject *II*.
    1. A smaller subject, part of *A*.
    2. A parallel small subject, related to *1* and part of *A*.

a. A subordinate subject that is part of 2.
b. Another subordinate idea, related to *a* in support of 2.
B. A second subordinate topic, parallel to A, part of main subject *II*.

A glance at this outline shows the writer that subject *A*, subordinate to main subject *I* has not been planned out fully enough. To achieve a balanced essay, plan out each section to within one logical step of the other parallel section. In section *I*, *A* is parallel to *B*, but *B* is planned out to *1* and *2*. What of *B* in main section *II*? How does it compare with its parallel member, *A*? Although *A* of *I* may be left as it is, *B* of *II* clearly needs further planning to make it more nearly balanced against *A* of *II*.

Are There Any Basic Rules for Outlining?

The major command is to fulfill the logical axiom: there is no *A* without a *B*. The reason for this is simple. Any subheading is only a part of its major heading. Therefore, there must be at least one other part to make up the whole of the major heading. *A* is not all of *I*, but only part of it. There must be at least a *B*, and there might be many other parts as well.

A second basic rule of outlining is that parallel ideas are placed beneath one another to make parallel items visible immediately. Finally, most teachers insist that outlines be consistently either sentence outlines or topic outlines (expressed in phrases, without complete sentences). An outline of a student's nonresearch paper on "Student Apathy" might go something like this:

STUDENT APATHY

I. School conditions need reform.
   A. School corridors require reforms.
      1. The littered corridors need cleaning up.
      2. The walls covered with posters need regularizing.
         a. A restricted area should be set aside for posters.
         b. Posters should be kept within a certain size.
   B. The conditions of the cafeteria require reforms.

1. The expensive food should be cheaper.
2. The diet offered should be balanced.
3. Acoustical tiles should be put on the ceiling to cut down the noise.

C. The curriculum also needs reform.
  1. More electives should be offered.
  2. Most of the required courses should be made optional.
  3. Many courses, unchanged for twenty years, should be improved.

II. Students show little interest in correcting these conditions.
  A. Students are unwilling to run for elective office.
    1. They say that they cannot have active social lives and serve the community too.
    2. They say that they are preparing actively for exams and must study.
    3. Some just refuse responsibility saying, "Let George do it."
  B. They do nothing constructive about cafeteria conditions.
    1. They complain about the food.
    2. They leave litter on the floor.
    3. They shout above the noise.
  C. They do nothing constructive about the corridors.
    1. They drop gum and cigarette wrappings on the floor.
    2. They write on the walls.
    3. Sometimes they vandalize.
  D. They are not interested in curriculum reform.
    1. They say they expect all books and classes to be dull.
    2. Many just wait until they can graduate and can get a job.
    3. Many do not know why they go to school.

III. What is the significance of student apathy?
  A. Does student apathy indicate that students willingly accept deplorable conditions?
    1. If they accept these conditions willingly, then there is no cause for concern.
    2. If they accept these conditions unwillingly, the situation is serious and should be remedied.
  B. Does student apathy indicate distrust of the school administration?
    1. Do some students think that improvements will not be undertaken, even if they are pointed out?
    2. Are some students discouraged by previous unfulfilled promises made by the administration?

C. Does student apathy indicate distrust of sustained student participation?
  1. Some students suspect that the student leaders support clean-up drives just to be elected as reform candidates.
  2. Some students fear that if they ran for office themselves, became elected, and could not sustain student interest in reforms, they would look weak and ineffective.
D. A school-wide analysis and discussion of apathy is necessary.
  1. Before any reforms can be initiated with hopes of remedy, the sources of apathy must be understood.
  2. Everyone at all levels—students, faculty, and administration—must be involved in order to effect reforms.
  3. Everyone at all levels must be involved for the reforms, once effected, to be sustained.
  4. Before the faculty and administration are involved, students must meet.
    a. We must discuss the problems that we see around us.
    b. We must discuss the reforms that we think are realistic.
    c. We must try to offer specific suggestions for constructive reform.
    d. If we can do all this, we will have started on our way out of student apathy.

That outline would serve a nonresearch paper, but the general pattern could be used for a library paper or a paper derived from research done outside a library. If your data is gathered from interviews, observations, newspapers, magazine articles, or books, the same principles of parallelism, order, and logic hold.

How Should I Work from Outline to Writing?

Whether you are writing a short paper from a firm outline—what's wrong with children's TV, what it should be, some suggestions to improve it—or a long research paper in which the outline has been drawn out of your notes, a central writing problem remains: to soften that outline. You will be aiming for clarity, but you don't want your reader to hear you marching from *Ia* to *Ib*. Suppose you transcribed literally *Ia* from the "Student Apathy," outline:

School corridors need reform. The littered corridors need cleaning up. The walls covered with posters need regularizing. A restricted area should be set aside for posters. All posters should be kept within a certain size.

The bare bones are showing. Your awareness of transitional elements and amplification need to be engaged:

Any visitor to the school knows that the corridors need reform [A 1]. Litter of all sorts needs cleaning up. [Here, expand and list the kinds you have seen.] Part of the disorder comes from posters of all sizes hanging crazily at all angles. [Expansion follows.] Some face the visitor to the auditorium, the gymnasium, the men's room, the laboratory, the stair landings, even the drinking fountains. Although I do not boast about the neatness of my dresser drawers, I do resent being sold something or someone everywhere I look. My eye can't rest on a blank wall without seeing: "Movies Saturday night—Mad, Violent, Wonderful"; or "Vote for Josie, the best School-Treasurer ever!" [A 2 a]. If a particular area were set aside for posters, then people would plan to go there to get the news, instead of being bopped by surprise at every waste basket or stair landing. Since everyone would stop by regularly to review the latest poster, the eyecatcher would be not necessarily the size of the posters, but their color and cleverness of design [A 2 b]. Then they could be kept within a certain size to permit everyone to advertise who wants to. Some people will say that you cannot sell a product without repetition. When people do not wish to listen, that is true. But ten minutes of real attention by people wanting the news is worth twenty-five guerrilla attacks by slogans on the ceiling. Of course, the corridors will still be school corridors; they can't be transformed into the Big Rock Candy Mountain, but anyone would agree that eliminating the litter from the floors, walls, and ceilings would help the view.

You will work through your paper in this fashion, amplifying or developing the basic points listed in your outline, although that tough-guy tone might not be your choice.

It might help to see a student at work on her outline. Here is Sue Chin's first outline on "The Generation Gap":

A. My own experiences
  1. Education
    a. Parents' hopes versus self-doubt
    b. Pressure
  2. Social
    a. Overprotection
      1. Only girl
      2. "Daddy's little baby"
    b. Friends
      1. Impressions parents have
    c. The Boy
      1. My ideal, as compared to parents'

Here is her revision of that outline.

THE "GENERATION GAP"

I. Definition: mostly alienation of child from parents (or vice versa) due to differences in opinion concerning:
  A. Education.
    1. Parents expectations and hopes versus child's self-doubt and personal desire.
    2. Pressure applied by parents for higher grades.
  B. Economic.
    1. Child's wish to work for more economic freedom.
    2. A job as the first symbol of "leaving the nest."
  C. Social.
    1. Child's awareness of a whole new world: new friends, new educational and occupational opportunity.
    2. Parent's notion of "their little baby"—forever.
      a. Leading to overprotection.
      b. Leading to meddling, invasion of child's privacy.
    3. Friends.
      a. Impressions of their child's companions, especially those of the opposite sex.
      b. Child's basic need for people his own age.
II. Possible solutions.
  A. On the part of the child:
    1. Understanding that parents do love him.
    2. Using tact and maturity to quiet parents' fear, and yet remaining free to grow.
    3. Learning the true meaning of growing up.
      a. Growing up, not just being old enough to leave home.
      b. Growing up to new opportunities and responsibilities.

159

B. On the part of the parents.
  1. Understanding that a child needs more than just parental love and protection.
  2. Understanding that giving a child his freedom doesn't mean losing him.
  3. Understanding that too much love can strangle and drown a child.

Compare Sue Chin's first three paragraphs with the second outline as revised to see the way she avoids sounding as if she is marching from roman numeral *I* to letter *A*, and so forth.

The term "generation gap" has been defined, talked about, and analyzed by the leading psychologists of our time. But the people who probably know the most about the "generation gap" are the parents and the children themselves. The generation gap is mostly the alienation of a child from his parents (or vice versa) because of differences in opinion concerning the child's educational, economic, and social life.

Parents have a natural tendency to have high hopes and expectations for their children. But often these hopes and expectations exceed the child's own capabilities, and, at times, his own personal desires. My own parents have high hopes of my earning a doctorate in biology. But sometimes I have my own little self-doubts. I often feel pressured "to get straight A's" or to do more work. It is hard to make a loving parent understand that there is a limitation to their child's capabilities.

But often school is just one of the problems a growing (and maturing) child faces. Sometimes a child reaches a certain point in his life when he feels the need for more economic freedom. He wants to be able to buy something without thinking, "Well, it's my dad's money." So he gets a job after school. But often parents mistake this gesture for economic freedom as the first sign of their child's leaving the nest.

This freshman is already using techniques of the transitional word, such as "but, so" and the repeated word or phrase—"capabilities," "these hopes," "economic freedom"—in order to soften the outline and smooth out her writing.

reviewing your own paper

How Can I Give My Paper a Last Review Myself?

First, in reviewing your own paper, try to be objective and to derive all your understanding from the words you read. Try not to remember what you meant when you wrote the words. Try using these review questions.

INTRODUCTION

Does the introductory paragraph or paragraphs cover the whole paper? Put another way, can everything in the paper be said to develop from this introduction? Is the introduction expressed abstractly enough to cover all the paper's subjects? Is there anything in the paper that does not, in some way, relate to the introduction? Does the last sentence in the introduction focus firmly on the central theme of the paper?

TOPIC SENTENCES

Read off the topic sentences of each paragraph. Do they proceed logically? Are there any logical gaps or jumps between paragraphs that might require transitions or a rearrangement of paragraphs? Can the existing jumps be corrected by improved transitional words or phrases?

PARAGRAPHS

Where might the paragraph that now seems out of place be put to serve best the logical sequential development? Do the paragraphs move toward more-and-more important ideas? Are all the paragraphs about the same length? Would some seem easier for the reader if they were divided? Look for the hinge in the paragraphs where emphasis shifts: "But strictly speaking, this does not apply to . . . ." Could the paragraph be divided there?

DOCUMENTATION

Is there a footnote number at the end of every sentence or passage (quoted or not) that contains an idea that you did not have before you began research? Are all words and phrases that are not your own surrounded by quotation marks? Ideas paraphrased and expressed entirely in the writer's words and phrases should not be quoted, but if taken from someone else's work they should be footnoted. If a quoted passage is set within a larger paragraph that is footnoted as a whole, the quotation need not be footnoted separately, provided the footnote cites the page reference that applies to the quotation as well as to the larger paragraph. Have you checked each footnote for accuracy of page number and quotation?

CONCLUSION

Does the conclusion mention all the paper's major points? Can they be reviewed and expressed in some refreshing fashion: by a comparison, by repetition of an early theme or idea, by an anecdote, or by a quotation? Does the tone of the conclusion seem to suit the paper and its progression as a whole?

CONTENT

Are all your generalizations supported by "evidence"? In the research paper the evidence might be taken from history, interviews, literature, legal cases; in informal or nonresearch papers the evidence might be merely personal opinions and personal experience, but both the formal and informal essays absolutely require illustrations and support for all generalizations. Have you said what you meant—fully? Are there places that need fuller explanation, fuller development, for clarity?

PACE

Does your paper seem to whiz along from introduction toward conclusion? Few papers do, but that is the ideal—to give a detective story pace to the essay. Have you cut out all fillers, all padders, all extra adjectives and adverbs, all lumpy clauses? Have you used the right word always, not the impressive or fancy or vague word? Have you eliminated or rewritten all clichés? Do sentences have the transitional elements they need to permit them to move swiftly forward in clear, logical relationship to one another? If you read your paper and have the sense that it moves rapidly and almost inevitably toward its conclusion, you will be pleased with yourself, and you should be.

This Seems Like a Lot of Work to Write a Paper. Is It Really Worth It?

This business of writing papers will become a strange kind of pleasure for you—"strange" only because writing always remains difficult. If the effort of a sport gives you pleasure, you can see how writing becomes intensely interesting too. With all the sweating, fatigue, and muscle strain, the person who loves a sport enjoys the effort it takes to serve or tackle or swim. Why? That's a question worth trying to answer. The effort to analyze, to choose the precise word that expresses a shade of meaning, to organize so that the paragraphs race toward their conclusion, that effort is to the writer what concentration on foot or shoulder position, or on angles, or speed or stroke is to the tennis player or golfer or rider or swimmer. The scene may not be so dramatic to the viewer watching you at your desk, but you know that the inner drama is lively.

The effort to analyze your own thinking is deeply interesting for its own sake, but its results are cumulative as well. The more frequently you write and make that effort to say precisely what you mean, the more habitual those analytical techniques will become. Frequent writing develops better writers, of course, but it also develops habits of thought. Life becomes more deeply lived as its instants are considered and reconsidered. In fact, it is a wonderfully cumulative and interrelated process that connects writing with self-knowledge and understanding of others. It might be expressed like a lovely problem in addition: the more you write, the more you analyze, the more you understand, the more you sympathize, the more you live.

scenes from your autobiography

All of these considerations of language lead to the self and out again toward understanding of others and back in a never-ending loop of consciousness. This small book about the mind of the writer began with the image of the mirror, with writing considered as a mirror into which the writer gazes to find himself. Writing is no self-congratulating mirror, aided by soft lights and actor's makeup. It is informative, not always pleasing. "Give me that glass, and therein will I read," Shakespeare's Richard II said, reaching for the mirror to help self-discovery. All the discussions of writing, reading, language, listening of these pages have presumed that the point of it all is self-discovery, and by consequence, the discovery of others. All of these labors in and out of school lead to, or should be aimed toward, growing awareness and understanding of that multiplicity called "self" and the variety called "others." Obviously, these concerns should never stop, no matter how few or how many degrees you earn.

Students say, "What's it all about?" and the inevitable answer is "Your life." One of the primary assumptions of this book is that you can teach yourself better than anyone else can. Teachers offer experiments, ideas, or processes to try out and to think through. In the thinking process, qualitative changes take place that no one can give you; you create them for yourself. In this sense, each person is responsible for his or her own growth; each person civilizes himself. In Hesse's novel *Siddhartha* the wise father, Siddhartha, could not supply his son with his own understanding, the product of his own growth. He could only step aside, finally, and permit the boy to grow in his own way. The great teacher can be your own autobiography.

How Do I Go About Writing an Autobiography? It Sounds Like Building a Monument.

Avoid the "soup to nuts" autobiography that begins with your ancestors and gets you born after fifty pages. Rather, consider the project as scenes from your autobiography. Do not try to write a thorough record, but write short essays of scenes. Use insights or themes as your focus, for example, the theme of your growing independence. Can you recall the time you realized that your parents were not all-powerful or might be hurt by you? When did you first begin to learn to be independent? How did you learn to stand up for yourself or to be yourself? How was that realization phrased in your mind in childhood language? Select a major theme for discussion in an essay about your own growth or development. You might consider the change in your attitudes toward one of these subjects: "friendship," "family parties," "religious worship." You might use the familiar essay instead of the formal exposition as your genre.

What Is the Familiar Essay?

The familiar essay, as distinct from the more formal exposition, is the fairly unstructured form made famous by Michel de Montaigne (see pp. 127-130). His introductions are casual; they barely introduce the topic. His conclusions are often nonexistent. He rambles, offering many interesting insights, with illustrations drawn from the ancients, from nature, from history, from wherever his broad-ranging interests have carried him. Generally speaking, Montaigne's technique is to treat themes like "How Our Mind Hinders Itself," "Cowardice, Mother of Cruelty," "Of the Resemblance of Children to Fathers," "Of the Greatness of Rome." His graceful and thoughtful essays written in the sixteenth century still make a reader respond in sympathetic understanding;

> I seek in books only to give myself pleasure by honest amusement; or if I study, I seek only the learning that treats of the knowledge of myself and instructs me in how to die well and live well.[4]

> I am not afraid to admit that my nature is so tender, so childish, that I cannot well refuse my dog the play he offers me or asks of me outside the proper time.[5]

If you note the titles of the essays from which these selections were taken—"Of Books" and "Of Cruelty"—you can suppose how informal, how unstructured the essays seem. Their intimacy is not the result of Montaigne's specific revelations but of general ones. Montaigne does not, in our contemporary manner, overwhelm his reader with specific examples of lapses in control or taste; rather his analysis plunges far deeper and says, in one sense, far more about humankind in general:

> I see this evident, that we willingly accord to piety only the services that flatter our passions. There is no hostility that excels Christian hostility. Our zeal does wonders when it is seconding our leaning toward hatred, cruelty, ambition, avarice, detraction, rebellion. Against the grain, toward goodness, benignity, moderation, unless as by a miracle some rare nature bears it, it will neither walk nor fly.[6]

Montaigne's calm, lucid honesty is quite clear from these examples. And whether you choose to write using many specific and concrete examples or to try to express general truths in Montaigne's manner, the value of your autobiography for yourself will depend on how rigorous your attempt is to be accurate or honest.

Is the Approach by Themes the Only Way to Write About My Own Life?

You may enjoy writing the direct narrative or group of descriptions, in the manner of "scenes from childhood," more than the thematic approach. Reading some autobiographical sketches would give you a sense of recreating a scene. A sentence like this suggests how concrete details will evoke a time and a scene: "I was eleven years old, a seventh-grader, when I was first shown into the big study hall in Forest Ridge Convent and issued my soap dish, my veil, and my napkin ring."[7] Those three precise details create more than a scene. They suggest atmosphere and manners, a world in which the three pillars of life were cleanliness, religion, and the courtesies of the dining table. Let yourself be that specific, precise, and selective.

You may think that your own life was just the usual ordinary life, but precise details remembered seem to make every life remarkable. Can you recall the look and smell of the kitchen as dinner was cooking? Who was present during dinner? Where did you sit? Did you watch TV during dinner? Was dinner a pleasant time, or was it the time for family arguments? Did you ever walk out on the family at dinner, or were you sent from the table? Were you expected to eat everything on your plate? Was there always enough? Prod your own memories to try to recall those years. One usually recalls events of childhood casually, without scrutiny, but try to reinterpret one of those remembered scenes now. Some of the simplest childhood events have interest and a new interpretation when retold by the more mature mind. The memory tape seems to remain in the mind, ready for replaying whenever we choose:

> With the help of some grown-up person, who would use first both hands and then a powerful leg, the divan would be moved several inches away from the wall, so as to form a narrow passage which I would be further helped to roof snugly with the divan's bolsters and close up at the ends with a couple of its cushions. I then had the fantastic pleasure of creeping through that pitch-dark tunnel, where I lingered a little to listen to the singing in my ears—that lonesome vibration so familiar to small boys in dusty hiding places—and then, in a burst of delicious panic, on rapidly thudding hands and knees I would reach the tunnel's far end, push its cushion away, and be welcomed by the sunshine on the polished floor and by a cloud of flowers.[8]

The well-remembered details make this scene vivid, the way the divan was moved, "first both hands and then a powerful leg," his listening to the "singing" in his ears, the precision of the phrasing, "on rapidly thudding hands and knees" and the "sunshine on the polished floor." It is, too, sentimental in its phrasing, as the author remembers childhood (perhaps too sweetly?), the "fantastic pleasure of creeping," the panic described as "delicious," and the verb "welcomed" followed by the dreamy "cloud of flowers." Your own remembrance of childhood may be much more rugged and much less sugary, but to recall it as accurately as you can is worth your effort.

And what about the person of this moment, with a mind full of new ideas and new impressions, or numb from being bombarded by too much from TV, radio, music, portable transistors, newspapers, posters, and what not? Can writing help that person focus this welter of impressions? Sometimes it is best to be still, to rest, to listen to nothing or to the sounds that float up from where people are coming back from work or from school, talking or washing dishes. But sometimes you may wish to order your impressions; then writing can help. Try to forget how it sounds, but aim first to get "it" said, articulated as precisely as possible. There is an ordering and an analyzing that takes place in the process of articulation that is helpful. You may wish to keep a journal, not the sort of steamy journal that smaller brothers and sisters love to discover, but a helpful one nonetheless.

There are basically three kinds of autobiographical writing that might be of use to you: the writing that aims to recreate early moments of living, the confessional writing that expresses for the page what can not be expressed to a friend, and the analytical writing that traces themes of development. These can be mixed, blended, separated in any combination, but essentially these are the basic ingredients. The perceptions of the world about, of other people, of customs, give autobiographical writing added interest for others, but this autobiography is for yourself, and you must follow your judgment about what will make it useful for you.

How Could I Start Writing My Autobiography?

A more methodical approach to writing your autobiography might get it started more easily than these mentioned. What are the institutions that are believed to touch every citizen to some degree? They would include representatives of the family, church or synagogue, schools, government, business, and medicine. In a page of exposition devoted to each, present your ideas on these institutions. For example, what are your attitudes toward the family as an institution? What function does it serve? Does it seem to be established for the help of each member? Do you have questions about its value as an institution? If you find that one of those institutions listed above seems to touch your life hardly at all, or that you have no thoughts about it, consider that fact. Why is it that you have no opinion about doctors and medicine or no idea about the government's relation to you?

Writing makes visible to the writer those shapeless places in his head. Teachers can ask students to ask questions, but if you do not know what you do not know, how can you shape a question? As you face a page that expresses your own values about religion and the family, the obvious question to ask yourself is: "Why do I think this way? Why do I have these particular values, these particular opinions of the way to live? Are there others I might have had?" A book like James Houston's *White Dawn,* which describes the living of the Eskimos so vividly, and makes the mind reel by its view of the white man seen through the mind of an Eskimo, forces the reader to recognize his own provinciality. Most people hold the views they do because their parents held them. Is that why you have the views you do about those primary institutions just named? If your views depart from those of your family, do you know why they do? Do you have reasons for your own views? For example, could you defend logically, with sound reasons and facts, your attitude about American business?

The long, interwoven line of research, logic, introspection, and writing techniques closes in a ring upon itself. Your present values about any one of those powerful institutions need deepening—anyone's do—and out of your reading and research will come a new stage of enlightenment. This network of new views should be articulated for yourself and probably for others as well. How persuasively you articulate these views will depend upon your grasp of research skills, techniques of organization, control of those matters of word choice, style, and tone, and the choices you make as you face your audience considering those three weights: audience, self, and subject.

Anyone gasps at the problem of holding those variables in

control. Libraries could be filled with books describing how to treat each of the elements listed in that forty-five-word summary sentence. But consider one last idea, one that these pages assume and will finally rest upon. In these months and years, the process, not the product, is the goal of your labors. It would be glorious if the young writer could produce *War and Peace* or *Moby Dick* before he was twenty, but it is not expected. Those giant novels were written by men in their thirties. Still, this process of reading, introspection, and writing permits and nurtures development, and the growing process is what schooling is about. What truly aids that process is to be encouraged; what hinders it is to be avoided. The importance of your autobiography is not that all this happened to the young Albert Schweitzer or the young Madame Curie, but that it happened to a unique human creature who witnessed a particular confluence of moments and events. It does not matter now whether or not you go on to win the Nobel prize. That will matter later. At this moment it is the process that counts—the process that nurtures humaneness, increases your awareness of self, and stimulates your intelligent response to others, to what they have written and what they appear to say. That growth process is worth your time. In fact, this kind of growth may be the only thing worth anyone's time. And writing will help you with that process.

NOTES FOR PART 3

Both the form shown here and the form shown on p. 150 are correct for a footnote page. Use the form preferred by your instructor.

1. Philip Thody, ed., *Albert Camus: Lyrical and Critical Essays,* trans. Ellen Conroy Kennedy (New York: Alfred A. Knopf, Inc., 1968), p. 336.

2. Albert Camus, "Preface to *The Stranger,*" in *Lyrical and Critical Essays,* ed. Thody, pp. 335–36.

3. Lynn White, Jr., *Medieval Technology and Social Change* (New York: Oxford Univ. Press, 1968), pp. 125–6.

4. Michel de Montaigne, "Of Books," *The Complete Essays of Montaigne,* ed. and trans. Donald Frame (New York: Doubleday, 1960), II, 83.

5. Montaigne, "Of Cruelty," ed. Frame, II, 111.

6. Montaigne, "Apology for Raymond Sebond," ed. Frame, II, 120.

7. Mary McCarthy, "A Memory of a Catholic Girlhood," in *Writing About Oneself,* ed. Robert Garis (Boston, Mass.: D.C. Heath, and Company, 1965), p. 98.

8. Vladimir Nabokov, "Speak, Memory," in *Writing About Oneself,* ed. Garis, p. 17.

glossary

ABSTRACTIONS An abstract term, or an abstraction, is a noun that generalizes about particulars. Greenness is an abstraction that refers to the color of grass, hemlock trees, most shrubs. Truth, loyalty, belief, feudalism, bigotry, corruption are abstractions drawn from observation of these qualities in individual events.

ALLITERATION The sound effect that results from the repetition of initial consonants in consecutive or neighbor words like bean bag, three toed toad, or: With mighty maces the bones they broke/ He through the thickest of the throng thrust/ Where stumble steeds strong and down go all . . . . Chaucer, *Knight's Tale*.

BIBLIOGRAPHY The study of all non-authorial aspects of making a book: its paper, type, print, binding and history. The term also refers to lists of books and articles written on a subject.

BODY OF PAPER That section between the introduction and the conclusion comprised by the middle paragraphs.

CLASSIFICATION A technique of paragraph development in which the subject of the paragraph is divided into parts and each part is discussed separately within the paragraph. The paragraph might develop this sentence: "There are three kinds of letters home: fond ones, angry ones, and evasive ones." Bacon's famous "Of Studies" begins: "Studies serve for pastimes, for ornaments, for abilities . . . ."

CLICHÉ A stale conventional word or phrase, for example, "He sought high and low to help those less fortunate than himself"; or "In these troubled times it behooves us to address ourselves to improving the quality of life."

CONCLUSION The paragraph or paragraphs at or near the end of the paper in which the major points of the paper are restated or summarized.

CONNOTATION Refers to the emotional atmosphere that a word carries, not to its explicit or dictionary meaning. The emotional quality found in a word differs between individuals. Crisp, Miami, library, bell—each word has a definite meaning but each carries widely different associations, or connotations, for different people.

CONTEXT The setting, the verbal environment of the word, phrase, sentence, or passage being considered. The context of this definition is the glossary of a student handbook.

DECLARATIVE SENTENCE   A sentence which states or asserts, does not question, command, or suppose is declarative.

DENOTATION   A word's explicit or dictionary meaning, not what it suggests, implies, or connotes.

ELLIPSIS   The omission of words or phrases understood in speech but indicated in writing by three spaced periods.

FOCUS   This term borrowed from photography is used in composition to refer to clarity of perspective: "This paper needs focus," a central point. (See thesis.) As a verb in, "You need to focus this paper," the writer is asked to bring clarity of attitude or thesis to his paper. If a paragraph has a clear subject that it supports soundly without wandering, it has focus.

INDENTATION IN PARAGRAPH DIVISION   The ten-space or two-word recess at the beginning of a line, a signal as important as capitalization, punctuation, or word choice in written communication. It indicates the beginning of a new idea-unit, or paragraph, and should be used judiciously.

METAPHOR   An implied comparison in which the qualities of one object are applied to another without using "like" or "as," for example: "In the gale winds the small boat bucked and reared," is a metaphor which compares the boat to a horse.

NEW JOURNALISM   A term applied to the work of those contemporary writers for the press who avoid the appearance of objectivity and write as personal witnesses to their time in the "I-was-there" manner.

PARAGRAPH   A subdivision of a larger composition indicated by indenting. A written passage that is unified about one developed idea.

PLAGIARISM   The action of taking another person's words or ideas and presenting them as one's own. Plagiarism in writing is avoided by the use of quotation marks and footnotes which credit the source of the words or ideas being used.

POINT OF VIEW   A literary term that refers to the mind through which the events described are viewed. The author may choose, among other possibilities, to write from the point of view of one character, to shift from one point of view to another, or to write from the omniscient point of view, by which he appears to know all the actions and motivations of all the characters. He may choose a trustworthy or naïve or deceptive character, or he may choose to tell the story objectively and still restrict all described to what one character might conceivably perceive.

PROCEDURAL TRANSITION   Transitions which state the way the writer plans to proceed: "Before discussing X we should first consider Y." These transitions are boring, unnecessary and avoidable.

PROSE   Broadly speaking, language written or spoken that is sequential (but not a list) and that does not have a patterned rhythm, although good prose may have a subtle and varied rhythm.

RESTRICTIVE CLAUSE   A clause necessary for the identification of the noun it modifies; it is not separated off by commas, for example: "The dog *that is trotting* *down the street* likes fish." "Most people *who like to travel* are adventurous."

SIMILE A direct comparison (not an implied one) in which a resemblance is found between two dissimilar things: "The unpleasant idea remained, like a stone in the shoe, until she could empty her mind of it."

SLANTING A non-objective writing technique by which the writer leads the reader to feel and think as the writer wishes by careful choice of emotionally loaded words.

STYLE Refers to the writer's word choice which creates a style: smooth, casual, formal, journalistic, simple, precise, awkward, uneven. It is impossible to write in no style. Essentially, the style should suit the purpose.

STYLE MANUAL A text that prescribes correct footnote and bibliography form, not correct "style" in word choice.

TAUTOLOGY The unnecessary repetition of an idea in different words within a sentence: the basic fundamentals, the necessary essentials, exact same, very unique, big huge.

THESIS STATEMENT The central idea of an essay expressed usually in the introduction by the so-called thesis statement.

TONE The feeling or attitude that the author's words express. The author may "mean" or not to express bitterness, condescension, arrogance, or joy, but his words will carry some tone or emotional atmosphere.

TOPIC SENTENCE The sentence which expresses the central point of a paragraph. Although it usually appears as the first sentence of a paragraph, it may appear anywhere in a paragraph.

TRANSITIONS The words or phrases which link sentences and paragraphs and usually express some logical relationship between the elements connected: and, however, still, on the other hand, in addition to, similarly, consequently, as a result, in brief, in short, to sum up.

index

179